GREAT LIVES OBSERVED

Gerald Emanuel Stearn, *General Editor*

IN JESUS, HUGH ANDERSON PRESENTS TEXTUAL STUDIES OF JESUS' OWN WORDS BY LEADING SCHOLARS, INTERPRETATIONS OF HIS MINISTRY BY COMMENTATORS THROUGH THE AGES, AND A TWENTIETH-CENTURY UNDERSTANDING OF HIS SIGNIFICANCE AS AN HISTORICAL AND RELIGIOUS FIGURE, TO CREATE A THREE-FOLD PERSPECTIVE. THE BIOGRAPHY OF JESUS IS THE BIOGRAPHY OF A MAN AND OF A BELIEF. AS THE WRITINGS COLLECTED HERE INDICATE, IT IS ALSO THE BIOGRAPHY OF THE MEN AND THE GENERATIONS OF MEN THAT HAVE SHARED THAT BELIEF.

HUGH ANDERSON, *the editor of this volume in the Great Lives Observed series, is Professor of New Testament Language, Literature and Theology at the University of Edinburgh. He has served in chaplaincy work in Egypt and Palestine, as Lecturer in Hebrew at the University of Glasgow, and as minister of Trinity Church, Pollokshields, Glasgow. From 1957 to 1966 he was Professor of Biblical Criticism and Theology at Duke University, and held various Visiting Lectureships in colleges and universities in the United States. The author of a number of articles on both Old and New Testament subjects, he is also co-editor of* The New Testament in Historical and Contemporary Perspective. *His recent publications include* Historians of Israel (2) *and* Jesus and Christian Origins. A Commentary on Modern Viewpoints.

GREAT LIVES OBSERVED

JESUS

Edited by HUGH ANDERSON

"Love your enemies,
do good to those who hate you,
bless those who curse you,
pray for those who abuse you."

—LUKE 6:27-28

A SPECTRUM BOOK

PRENTICE-HALL, INC., ENGLEWOOD CLIFFS, N.J.

The author wishes to express his gratitude to Miss Florence M. Russell of New College, Edinburgh, for her generous help in assembling this collection.

Englewood Cliffs, New Jersey.

A SPECTRUM BOOK

Current printing (last number):

10 9 8 7 6 5 4 3

Library of Congress Catalog Card Number: 67-28396

Printed in the United States of America

Contents

PART TWO
NINETEENTH CENTURY LIBERAL VIEWS OF JESUS

PART THREE
JESUS IN THE TWENTIETH CENTURY

GREAT LIVES OBSERVED

JESUS

Introduction

In 1924 a considerable furor arose in France, and in fact throughout Europe, when the Frenchman P. L. Couchoud published a monograph, in which he sought to demonstrate that Jesus had never lived, that the story of his life was an entirely mythical fabrication, built up mainly out of Old Testament texts. The narrative of the crucifixion of Jesus, for instance, was invented on the basis of such Old Testament passages as Psalm 22:16-18: "Yea, dogs are round about me; a company of evildoers encircle me; they have pierced my hands and feet—I can count all my bones—they stare and gloat over me; they divide my garments among them, and for my raiment they cast lots."

The view that Jesus was a figure of mythical origins was not, of course, by any means new, but Couchoud appeared to have presented at least a scholarly case for it. Daily newspapers, magazines and journals carried leading articles on the subject. Passionate feelings were stirred, and the explosive debate on the issue began to subside only after the eminent French Protestant scholar, M. Goguel, furnished sound critical arguments against the Jesus-myth theory.

So far as one is aware, there has never since been any such outburst. Save for some fugitive anti-Jesus propaganda from behind the Iron Curtain, scarcely anyone today ventures to suggest that Jesus was not a real historical person. Yet, however secure the fact of Jesus' life as a piece of actual history, the question of the course and character of that life remains a subject of unending debate.

Our knowledge of any historical personage is finally dependent on the quantity, quality, and character of our primary sources. In the case of Jesus, almost our only primary sources, as we shall see, are the Gospels of Matthew, Mark, and Luke. Judged by our standards, these are short works; all three together are not as big as a relatively small modern book. As a result the historian of the life of Jesus has to labor under the handicap of a serious paucity of firsthand materials. But also, just because the Gospels represent a quite peculiar type of literature, they confront the historian with singularly difficult problems. Devoted study of these documents over the past two centuries and more has shown us ever more clearly that they are certainly not straightforward biographical accounts of Jesus, on the basis of which the historian can easily proceed at once to reconstruct Jesus' life story. Rather were the Gospels produced in a situation some time after the death and resurrection of Jesus, when he had become a new object of religious devotion. Although they do recall and hark back to his days on earth, they were written in fact from the standpoint of faith in Jesus as the Messiah or Christ of God. They were the products of that community of faith, the Christian Church, which both then and now has proclaimed Jesus as the one in whose words and deeds God once decisively spoke and acted.

Precisely the amalgam in our primary sources of faith's testimony to Jesus as Christ and Lord on the one hand, and historical reminiscence of his earthly career on the other, constitutes the most fundamental problem for would-be observers of the life of Jesus. We must learn to distinguish between what *faith* affirms about Jesus, and what *history* recounts. Faith's knowledge of Jesus as the supreme Self-revelation of God and historical knowledge of his ministry on earth (although not necessarily incompatible with each other) are not exactly the same thing, and may not simply be combined forthwith into a single viewpoint. If, for example, we take two statements about Jesus from the Apostles Creed, first "crucified under Pontius Pilate," and second "sitteth on the right hand of God the Father Almighty," and really think about them, we can recognize that they are not of the same order or category. The former is a historical statement and the latter a faith statement, and the historian as historian can no more be expected to verify or prove the latter than the man of faith as man of faith can be expected to provide exact factual details about the former.

If *faith* sees Jesus as the one exalted to the right hand of God the Father, *history* regards him from its own particular point of view. In a rather negligible and politically insignificant Eastern province of the Roman Empire, there appeared a man with a message of the imminent closure of world history through the direct intervention of God. He summoned certain men to be his followers. In God's name he addressed words of promise, warning, and demand to his hearers. He performed striking deeds and went about doing good by healing the sick and befriending the oppressed. Toward the end of a short public career he had a serious brush with the religious and political authorities in the Jewish capital of Jerusalem, and was executed in customary Roman fashion. The sequel was destined to change the shape of the history of the West. His disciples banded solidly together in the belief that after his death he had made a fresh start with them again, had been exalted to God's side, and would soon appear once more on the earth in triumph. They had become convinced that in this Jesus the last act in the divine drama of salvation had now been accomplished. This faith and this message they carried across the Roman Empire until at length their seemingly irresistible momentum won over a considerable part of the human race and threatened the throne of the Caesars itself.

Now the truth of the message—that in and with Jesus God's great hour had struck—the historian cannot confirm by means of historical investigation. What he may do, however, is to evaluate the context in which the march of the new religion took place, by enquiring how Christianity surpassed and outstripped other existing religious cults. For the task of investigating the rise and expansion of the Church the historian, as it happens, has at his disposal an infinitely richer stock of documentary material than he possesses for the life of Jesus, out of which the Christian movement took its start. The acute shortage of sources for Jesus' career (and the unique character of such few sources as we have) we may deem exceedingly unfortunate; but it is a fact we have to face, a fact, moreover, which helps to account for the amazing variety of modern estimates and pictures of Jesus. Where objective data are lacking, subjective judgment and imagination are liable to be given free play.

Jesus himself, we must remember, wrote nothing, nor was anything written about him while he was still alive. The secular literature of the early centuries of our era almost totally neglects him. Only a few historians of the Roman Empire, who stood near to Jesus' own time, Tacitus, Suetonius, and Pliny the Younger, give him at best a passing mention. Presumably, from what little they knew of it, they took Jesus' activity to be but a minor episode in a third-rate Roman province. On the Jewish side, the historian Josephus makes two references to Jesus in his *Antiquities* from around A.D. 95. The first is simply the briefest allusion to James "the brother of Jesus who was called Christ." The second speaks of one or two items of Jesus' life, of his condemnation by Pilate to death through crucifixion, and of his resurrection (and even this evidence is precarious, for Josephus' work at this point had most probably been revised by a Christian scribe). In addition, the Jewish Talmud, compiled in its Palestinian form early in the fifth century and its Babylonian form around the middle of the sixth century, has some polemical and derogatory remarks on Jesus. All this is very little grist for the historian's mill—only enough to testify that Jesus was a real historical person.

Adolf von Harnack (writing about A.D. 1900) was justified in observing that, aside from the Gospels of the New Testament, just about everything we know concerning Jesus' history and teaching "may easily be put on a small sheet of paper, so little does it come to." Despite the intriguing archaeological discoveries that have been made in the interval, Harnack's verdict of 1900 remains substantially true today. In the excess of enthusiasm created by the finding of the Dead Sea Scrolls in 1947, hasty and often extravagant conjectures were made about their immediate bearing upon Jesus and primitive Christianity. The Scrolls afforded evidence of a vital Jewish sect that had been in existence for over a century before Jesus' time and owed allegiance to a leader named the Teacher of Righteousness. Some were quick to maintain, in the rash of publicity that followed the first discovery, that in light of certain prominent features of the Dead Sea Sect or the Sect of Qumrân, both the life of Jesus and the appearance of the early Church could at last be explained as strictly historical phenomena. But meanwhile we have had some twenty years of patient critical sifting of the Scrolls and related manuscripts and literary fragments found in other caves in the neighborhood of Qumrân, as well as continuing archaeological investigation of the site of the monastery that housed the members of the Sect. The upshot is that a more sober assessment of the similarities and *dissimilarities* between the Sect of Qumrân and primitive Christianity now prevails. The structure and thought of the Qumrân community reveal a number of affinities with the organizational and cultic life of the early Church or with certain doctrinal or confessional expressions of the Gospel in the hands of Paul or John. To the actual history or person of Jesus, however, Qumrân offers us no direct means of access, but rather fills out for us the Jewish landscape against which Jesus lived and died. (More will be said on this later.)

The case is much the same with the forty or more Christian manuscripts, written in the Coptic language, recently discovered in Egypt. Among these are some "gospels," the Gospel of Truth, the Gospel of Philip and the Gospel of Thomas. None of these three "gospels" furnishes any account of Jesus' life. Only the Gospel of Thomas includes sayings of Jesus that bear any resemblance to his utterances as recorded in the Gospels of the New Testament. Even so, it hardly has any independent value as a source-book on Jesus, for it almost certainly derives ultimately from the tradition of Jesus' sayings contained in the New Testament Gospels, and so adds nothing to what they already provide.

Over and above these more recent discoveries there are in existence numerous fragments of other apocryphal "gospels," which have been known to us for quite a long time; the Gospel of the Nazaraeans, the Gospel of the Ebionites, the Gospel of the Hebrews, the Gospel of the Egyptians, and the Gospel of Peter are among the earliest of them. But not only are such apocryphal "gospels" of later date than the New Testament Gospels, they also display a style of narration that is much more flowery and fanciful; they look in fact like legendary embellishments of pieces of information about Jesus already furnished in a more sober and restrained way in the New Testament. The contrast between Mark's very reserved notice of the resurrection of Jesus (Mark 16:1-8) and the account in the apocryphal Gospel of Peter is instructive in this regard. Mark nowhere even attempts to describe the rising again of Jesus; the Gospel of Peter speaks of two young men entering the sepulchre and of three of them coming out, "two of them sustaining the other and a cross following them, and the heads of the two reaching to heaven, but that of him who was led of them by the hand overpassing the heavens."

For anything like trustworthy knowledge of the historical Jesus we are, in the last analysis, driven back upon the four Gospels of the New Testament. And even then we have to be content with a still further reduction of our primary sources. For although the author of the Gospel of St. John may have incorporated in his work an important historical strand of tradition about Jesus, it is generally conceded that he has used great freedom in transposing events into his own theological or religious key, and that, save on certain important points of chronology, he cannot be considered on a par with the other three Gospel writers as an authority on the history of Jesus.

For study of the life and teaching of Jesus we are left, therefore, with the Gospels of Matthew, Mark, and Luke. *Can we take these Gospels to be reliable historical reports?* The first three Gospels (commonly called the Synoptic Gospels because of their close literary interrelationships) were produced in the period from about A.D. 65 to 95. That is to say that a time of over thirty years elapsed from the death of Jesus around A.D. 30 to the writing of Mark, the first of the Synoptic Gospels, about A.D. 65. The materials on which Mark and the Synoptic writers who followed him drew for the compilation of their Gospels were the traditions of Jesus' words and deeds, which had first of all circulated by word of mouth among various Christian communities during the generation after his crucifixion. If we are to have any acquaintance at all with the problems of reconstructing Jesus' history, we have to form some impression of this interim era of oral tradition. In the course of oral transmission the Christian congregations kept alive those traditions of Jesus' sayings and acts which could be turned to practical use in meeting the varied situations of their daily lives, in preaching, in mission, in cult and liturgy. We should not be at all surprised to find that in this whole fluid process traditions about Jesus were steadily reshaped, adapted, and heightened in color, especially since those responsible for passing them on were every other day witnessing new converts won and new conquests made in the name of Jesus Christ their Lord.

In the years since the First World War, critical analysis of the Gospels has taken full account of the period of oral transmission of the tradition about Jesus before its fixation in writing. Criticism has in fact brought us today to a vantage point from which we can see that Matthew, Mark, and Luke are not historical works in the ordinary sense at all. They were not composed with the simple object of preserving the facts of Jesus' career as they actually happened. Rather such description of Jesus' work and words as they contain was primarily intended to awaken or corroborate faith in Jesus Christ as God's agent in redemption. The word "gospel" means "good news," and the Synoptic Gospels, no less than the Gospel according to John, state their facts only in such a way as to communicate the good news of God's mighty acts in Jesus Christ.

In terms of their chief aim to convey religious truth within a framework of historical narration, the Gospels constitute a type of literature that had no counterpart in the Graeco-Roman world.

Accordingly, from the perspective of the *historian* these writings leave a great deal to be desired. The reader of Mark's Gospel quickly gathers that the various narratives are quite loosely connected and that their positions may be interchanged without significantly altering the overall picture of Jesus' activity. The only important exception is the narrative of the passion and death of Jesus. Moreover, the stories told by the Synoptic writers leave great gaps in our knowledge of Jesus' life. Mark's record begins, so to speak, with the "end" of Jesus' days on earth, and confines itself to the brief span of his public ministry, which opens with his baptism by John at the Jordan. Matthew and Luke do offer us introductory reports of the birth and infancy of Jesus (and Luke includes further a separate note on the boy Jesus in the Temple at Jerusalem), but these are couched in Old Testament language, have a distinctly legendary ring, and are not referred to either by Jesus himself or by the Synoptic writers in the traditions relating to the public ministry.

The fact is that we know nothing or next to nothing of Jesus' history for the first thirty years of his life. The materials are insufficient for anything like a biography of Jesus, either in regard to the inward development of his personality or to the outward course of events in chronological sequence. Pious, and sometimes not so pious, imagination has, to be sure, often tried to fill in the gaps, but the impressionistic pictures painted by imagination are no substitute for genuine historical reconstruction. At most the historian may legitimately say some things *negatively* about the "hidden years" of Jesus' history by inference from what the tradition does in fact disclose of the character of his ministry and teaching in the final stage of his life. For instance, Jesus' manner of speech stands in marked contrast to the theological language of the Apostle Paul. Jesus expresses what he has to say about God and man and the world in the common language of everyday, of the sower and the reaper, the lord of the vineyard, the idle workman in the marketplace, the shepherd searching for his sheep, and so on. From this we may deduce that, unlike Paul, Jesus had most probably never been through the technical theological training of the rabbinical school. Or again, it seems likely that Jesus had no direct connection in his early years with an Essene-like movement of the separatist type represented at Qumrân, or if he did, was not unduly influenced by it. Jesus, as the traditions of his ministry show, was no separatist. He displayed none of the normal traits of the ascetic, but moved about freely in his surroundings in search of outcasts and sinners and ate with them; consequently he was accused of being "the friend of publicans and sinners" and "a glutton and winebibber." However, in trying to recover the "hidden years" of Jesus we are in a realm of very great uncertainty and have no documentation at our disposal. And sound historical procedure demands that we should not manufacture connections where there are none in the records or fill in gaps out of our own imaginings.

What is left to the historian then if he is forced to acknowledge that a biography of Jesus cannot be written? How are we to describe the history of a man whose life, save for its last year or two, is concealed from us both in its inward and outward progression? If the religious attitudes and insights of the Church in the period after the death of Jesus are imprinted to such an extent on the traditions of his words and deeds, how can we ever be sure of attaining positive knowledge of the actual facts of his career? Of course it is true to say that nearly all the documents available to the historian for the study of any individual of the past have been so stamped to some extent with the subjective experiences of those who are describing the events. It is true also that the ascription of divine attributes to human beings is not altogether without parallel. In some places Gautama was identified as a special Buddha; Alexander the Great was accorded divine honors; and the Roman emperors were officially regarded as gods.

These analogies, however, do not assist us much with the problem of the historical Jesus. Jesus of Nazareth and the primary sources relating to him present us with a very special case. He was believed, through his resurrection, to have made a fresh start with his disciples and to have come alive again, and until today has been the object of worship, or at least of reverence, by very many people.

In his famous work on *The Quest of the Historical Jesus,* Albert Schweitzer made this just observation:

> The problem of the life of Jesus has no analogue in the field of history. No historical school has ever laid down canons for the investigation of this problem, no professional historian

> has ever lent his aid to theology in dealing with it. Every ordinary method of historical investigation proves inadequate to the complexity of the conditions. The standards of ordinary historical science are here inadequate, its methods not immediately applicable. The historical study of the life of Jesus has had to create its own methods for itself.[1]

The historical study of the life of Jesus of which Schweitzer speaks is in fact, when contrasted with the age of the Christian religion itself, a comparatively new discipline. For some eighteen hundred years scarcely any critical attention was paid to the life of Jesus on earth. Throughout the centuries of the Church's great age of Dogma, Christian believers were not in a position to form a conception of the historical career of the man Jesus. Admittedly in those early authoritative credal statements in which the Church sought to define her faith, every effort was made to preserve intact the true humanity of Jesus, as in the Nicene Creed: "And was made man, and was crucified also for us under Pontius Pilate. He suffered and was buried." But, as Schweitzer points out, the human life was so deeply encased in the dogma of the two natures, the divine and the human in Christ, that it could not be historically grasped. Two conditions had to be met before the problem of Jesus could emerge as a strictly historical rather than merely religious or theological problem. First, the age-old preoccupation with the doctrine of the divine and human natures in Christ had to be shattered. Second, critical reflection on the sources had to arise. Not until the eighteenth century did signs of any such breakthrough really appear.

Before that, the leading figures of the Reformation in the sixteenth century, Luther, Calvin, and Zwingli continued to be engrossed with dogmatics. To take but one example, though Calvin could speak of the Gospels as "Histories," they were for him "history" only in the sense that they reliably declared how the Son of God was sent, took human flesh, and went about with men in this life. Whereas the Reformers were not altogether uncritical of the Scriptures, their critical attitudes did not yet involve the exercise of historical reason or historical method. Faced with the fact that in the Gospel of John Jesus' cleansing of the Temple is placed at

[1] A. Schweitzer, *The Quest of the Historical Jesus,* trans. W. Montgomery, (London, 1922), p. 6.

the beginning of his public ministry, and at the end of it in the Synoptic Gospels, Luther remarked that if a difficulty crops up in regard to the Holy Scripture and we are unable to solve it, we must simply let it alone. Yet in his own way Luther did anticipate a typical attitude of the more radical modern critics when he observed: "The Gospels follow no order in recording the acts and miracles of Jesus, and the matter is not, after all, of much importance." [2] In his "Gospel Harmony" published at Basle in 1537, the Reformed theologian Andrew Osiander contended that where a word or action of Jesus was reported two or three times in altered form in different Gospels, Jesus must have said or done the same thing two or three times over—there must have been, for instance, two cleansings of the Temple, and three raisings of Jairus' daughter from the dead.

However, the Protestant Reformers did make their own contribution, indirectly at least, to the later growth of the historical method as applied to the Gospels. By focusing attention on the Scriptures as the sovereign arbiter of Christian faith and life, they created a climate of general interest in the New Testament especially, in which the spirit of critical enquiry could begin to flourish. But they also called in question the supreme place ascribed to ecclesiastical tradition in the interpretation of Scripture within the Roman Catholic Church; and from there it was not such a big step to that later critical examination of all tradition, including the tradition of the New Testament itself, which had as its goal the understanding of the person to whom the tradition bore witness, Jesus himself.

In the end historical investigation of the life of Jesus took its rise from the growing revolt against the tyranny of dogma that characterized the intellectual life of several European countries in the eighteenth century. In France Voltaire revealed a keen critical acumen, for example, in his observations on the testimony of Josephus, the Jewish historian, to Jesus. More formative and decisive for the pioneering progress of German theology in the nineteenth century was the work of the Deists in England and the Rationalism of the Enlightenment in Germany.

Among the English Deists, John Locke, Matthew Tindal, and Thomas Chubb deserve special mention. Embarked upon the

[2] See Schweitzer, *op. cit.*, p. 13.

pursuit of a "reasonable Christianity" that might thwart the breakup of Christendom into an ever-growing number of churches, Locke was led to contrast sharply the simple and understandable message of Jesus with the obscure and complicated theologizing of Paul.

Tindal set out to prove that Christianity is but the expression of Natural Religion and that *reason* must decide between truth and error in the Scriptures. His sortie on behalf of Natural Religion and reason brought him to the discovery that Jesus as well as Paul and the early Church shared the conviction that the kingdom of God would come within their own lifetime. All of them were in error, for the kingdom of God did not come. Mistaken in this, they could be mistaken in many things—only reason must decide between truth and falsehood.

Chubb for his part also discerned that the message of Jesus had to do with the imminent coming of the kingdom of God. But more than that, he wished to distinguish between the private opinions of St. Paul and St. John on such subjects as the place of the Jews in God's scheme of salvation and the pre-existence of Christ with God (which are of no consequence for men's salvation), and the plain message of Jesus. "The private opinions of those who were appointed and sent out to preach his gospel to the world, were in many instances very abstruse, and much above the capacities of the common people. Whereas, the gospel which Christ preached to the poor, and which he gave in charge to his Apostles to the world, was plain and intelligible, and level to the lowest understanding as indeed it ought and must needs be." [3]

With all this, and not least with the distinction drawn between the simple teaching of Jesus himself and the doctrinal opinions expressed about him by such as Paul, the ancient dogmatic crust in which the historical life of Jesus had been so long encased was being crumbled and the ground broken for a deeper search for the man of Nazareth.

In Germany, in the latter part of the eighteenth century, with some prodding from the English Deists, other spades were getting busy. Hermann Samuel Reimarus (1694-1768), professor of Oriental languages at Hamburg, came through with the first treatise in systematic criticism of the story of Jesus. Not until after his death

[3] Thomas Chubb, *The True Gospel of Jesus Christ Asserted* (London, 1738), pp. 47-49.

were seven portions of his massive manuscript of four thousand pages published by Lessing under the title of *Fragmente des wolfenbüttelschen Ungenannten.*

"We are justified," says Reimarus, "in drawing an absolute distinction between the teaching of the Apostles in their writings and what Jesus Himself in his own lifetime proclaimed and taught." In the last fragment of his work, called *The Aims of Jesus and of His Disciples,* Reimarus argues that Jesus always remained essentially a Jew. By taking the terms "kingdom of God" and "Messiah" on his lips Jesus was only subscribing to the common Jewish usage of his day. He had no thought of founding a new religion. To his disciples he held out glowing hopes of the coming kingdom of God, but what that meant for him was that he should become the head of a reestablished independent Jewish national state. When this failed and Jesus perished, his disciples conjured up the vision of a Second Coming of the Messiah, guaranteed by a resurrection which they simply invented after stealing Jesus' body, and got rid of the difficulty of his death by giving it the significance of a spiritual redemption.

All this was of course greatly daring, and caused grievous offence. Reimarus was in fact far ahead of his time. Though his bold interpretation of the Gospel story patently read into the texts what is not there, the national-political character of the kingdom of God and the fraudulence of the disciples, he had nevertheless raised two very crucial points. First, he stressed how Jesus had kindled the hopes of his disciples by his proclamation of the coming kingdom of God. Second, he detected the capital importance of the development from Jesus to the life of the Church. A long time was to elapse before these points were probed again in any depth. To Reimarus Schweitzer pays this eloquent tribute: "The fact is there are some who are historians by the grace of God, who from their mother's womb have an instinctive feeling for the real. They follow through all the intricacy and confusion of reported fact the pathway of reality, like a stream which, despite the rocks that encumber its course and the winding of its valley, finds its way inevitably to the sea." [4] In his "instinctive feeling for the real," Reimarus so far outstripped his contemporaries as critic of the Gospel record that there was none to take up where he left off.

However, in the latter part of the eighteenth century, important

[4] A. Schweitzer, *op. cit.,* p. 25.

advances were made in other directions. In that period there began to arise questions about the sources and literary relations of the New Testament writings, especially the Gospels, which were largely to dominate the research of the nineteenth century. Long before, of course, the mind of the early Church and its opponents had been exercised by the difficulty of contradictions and discrepancies in the various Gospel accounts. Some time after A.D. 170 Tatian composed a harmony of the four Gospels called the *Diatessaron,* which was to become the "official" life of Jesus for the Syrian Church. Later St. Augustine considered the literary connections of the different Gospels and put forward the view that Mark is an abridgment of Matthew. But only in the second half of the eighteenth century was the real magnitude of the problem recognized. J. G. Herder, for example, saw the futility of trying to harmonize the Gospel of John with the Synoptic Gospels. He further reversed Augustine's view by holding up Mark as the foundation stone of the other Gospels. In Mark he discovered a relative friendliness toward the Jews, but in Matthew a growing hostility occasioned by the increasing rift between Christianity and Judaism. In the Gospels generally he detected not so much pure history, but a sacred epic of Jesus the Messiah built up around Old Testament prophecies. "He contributed much to the clearing up of ideas," says Schweitzer of Herder, "but by evading the question of miracle he slurred over a difficulty which needed to be faced and solved before it should be possible to entertain the hope of forming a really historical conception of the life of Jesus." [5]

To such early Rationalists as K. F. Bahrdt and K. H. Venturini it was left to make a frontal attack on the miraculous element in the Gospels. The title of Venturini's work, *A Non-supernatural History of the Great Prophet of Nazareth* (1800), is self-explanatory. A principal clue to the history of Jesus, Venturini maintains, is his adoption in early childhood by a secret Essene order or brotherhood. What look like miracles in the Gospels are in fact very often simply the mysterious comings and goings of the members of this secret society. Witness Venturini's account of the death and resurrection of Jesus. Having laid the body of Jesus on a bed of moss in the rock grave, Joseph of Arimathaea saw a happy omen in the blood still flowing from the wounded side, and sent word to the Essene Brethren.

[5] Schweitzer, *op. cit.,* pp. 36-37.

> They had a hold close by, and promised to watch over the body. In the first four-and-twenty hours no movement of life showed itself. Then came the earthquake. In the midst of the terrible commotion a Brother, in the white robes of the Order, was making his way to the grave by a secret path. When he, illumined by a flash of lightning, suddenly appeared above the grave, and at the same moment the earth shook violently, panic seized the watch, and they fled. In the morning the Brother hears a sound from the grave: Jesus is moving. The whole Order hastens to the spot, and Jesus is removed to their Lodge. Two brethren remain at the grave—these were the "angels" whom the women saw later. Jesus, in the dress of a gardener, is afterwards recognized by Mary Magdalene. Later, he comes out at intervals from the hiding-place, where he is kept by the Brethren, and appears to the disciples. After forty days he took his leave of them: his strength has been exhausted. The farewell scene gave rise to the mistaken impression of his Ascension.[6]

Even more systematically and ruthlessly was the supernatural factor in the Gospel stories demolished by the full-blown Rationalism of H. E. G. Paulus. The reader should compare the terse account of the Ascension given in the Book of Acts (1:9-11) with Paulus' version. Revived from the rigor caused by crucifixion through the coolness of the grave and the aromatic unguents of the burial rites, Jesus lived quietly for forty days. Near the end, he returned from Galilee, where he had spent part of the time with his followers, to Jerusalem.

> On the Mount of Olives, in the early sunlight, he assembled his own for the last time. He lifted up his hands to bless them, and with hands still raised in benediction he moved away from them. A cloud interposes itself between them and him, so that their eyes cannot follow him. As he disappeared there stood before them, clothed in white the two dignified figures who were really among the secret adherents of Jesus in Jerusalem. These men exhorted them not to stand waiting there but to be up and doing. Where Jesus really died they never knew, and so they came to describe his departure as an ascension. For all the "miracles" of Jesus there are likewise straightforward natural explanations—Jesus' walking on the

[6] See A. Schweitzer, *op. cit.*, p. 47.

> water was simply an illusion, for in the mist he walked along the shore and was taken for a ghost by the alarmed occupants of the boat.[7]

Now that the Gospel records had been brought to the bar of reason and of historical science, the way was prepared for the Life of Jesus movement that was to constitute a prominent feature of the intellectual life of Europe throughout the nineteenth century.

But the movement could hardly have progressed as it did without the help of source-criticism of the Gospels. Protracted and detailed investigation of the written sources used by the Evangelists led gradually to the firm conclusion that among the Synoptic Gospels Mark was basic and primary, and that Matthew and Luke each made his own use of Mark together with a document consisting of collected sayings of Jesus, to which modern scholarship has given the name of Q (from the German *Quelle*=source). The Q document so-called did not of course survive separately—its existence is a scholarly hypothesis built up from the fact that a considerable number of sayings of Jesus are reported by Matthew and Luke with an almost verbatim similarity, and so presumably they were employing a common source.[8]

At any rate the growing establishment of the priority of Mark was very fruitful for the Life of Jesus movement. The earliest and foundational Gospel seemed to provide a reliable account of the ministry of Jesus in chronological or causal sequence, and could safely be taken as furnishing the data for a full-scale biographical reconstruction. On this view, Mark's record was meat and drink to those engaged on the quest who considered their task to be the cataloguing of the facts of Jesus' life "as they actually happened." Of late the fashion has been to draw a sharp contrast between the scientific or objective ideal of nineteenth-century historical study and the ideal of passionate self-involvement prevalent among twentieth-century historians. Thus James M. Robinson writes: "The positivistic understanding of history as consisting of brute facts

[7] See A. Schweitzer, *op. cit.*, p. 55.

[8] Recently such scholars as Dom B. Butler, A. W. Farrer and W. R. Farmer have sought to refute the Q hypothesis. But the prevailing consensus of scholarly opinion still supports it, although some critics now allow that Q is highly speculative in character, and argue that we should think of it not as a clearly defined written document, but as a stage or layer of the oral tradition of Jesus' words.

gave way to an understanding of history centring in the profound intentions, stances, and concepts of existence held by persons in the past, as the well-springs of their outward actions." [9]

Robinson's picture in contrasts is almost certainly overdrawn and fails to do justice to the variety and fluidity of attitudes to history to be found in both centuries.[10] All the same he has properly drawn attention to the distinct tendency among the nineteenth-century historians of Jesus to aim at a biography in the sense of an orderly presentation of the objective data of his life. Whether they succeeded in being objective or whether they did not often give free play to their own subjective judgment and their own imagination is another question.

All the Gospel materials bearing on the life of Jesus were so assiduously studied by liberal Protestant theologians that within the space of a few generations, some sixty thousand biographies, so it is estimated, had been produced. Who of sufficient range of intellect and breadth of vision is to survey and measure an enterprise so massive, to bring some order into the chaos of the Lives of Jesus? In the earliest years of the present century the man for the task proved to be a young Alsatian of quite extraordinary talents, whose later exploits in an African jungle were to make his name a household word in the civilization he had left behind. We have alluded already to Albert Schweitzer's *The Quest of the Historical Jesus*. Within its pages, the most illustrious and influential of the Lives, perhaps notably those of David Friedrich Strauss and Ernest Renan, are both brilliantly described and trenchantly criticized.

The agony and the ecstasy of the quest Schweitzer clearly sensed. "The critical study of the life of Jesus has been for theology a school of honesty. The world has never seen before, and will never see again, a struggle for truth so full of pain and renunciation as that of which the Lives of Jesus of the last hundred years contain the cryptic record." [11] But no less clearly did Schweitzer see and expose the fundamental errors inherent in the attitude and approach of the liberal scholars. Having turned to the Jesus of history as an ally in the struggle against the tyranny of dogma, they made a concerted drive to push past the dogmatic element in Jesus' teaching. His

[9] James M. Robinson, *A New Quest of the Historical Jesus* (London, 1959), p. 39.

[10] Cf. James Barr, *Old and New in Interpretation* (London, 1966), p. 177.

[11] Schweitzer, *op. cit.*, p. 5.

strange apocalyptic, coming-end-of-the-world ideas, his proclamation of the imminent future coming of the kingdom of God; these must simply be understood as the outer first-century shell in which his true message was encased. Once extract the kernel, and the true message of Jesus could be seen to be of timeless value, at once understandable and relevant to the world of respectable, contemporary society. So, as Schweitzer understood it, in the nineteenth-century Lives a "Jesus for today" came to supplant the historical Jesus of the Gospel records, who is "to our time a stranger and an enigma." These portraits of Jesus were in fact highly subjective and fanciful modernizations, in which in turn the idealist, rationalist, socialist, or romanticist created his hero in conformity with his own aspirations.

Sharply and all as Schweitzer rapped the composers of the liberal Lives, he did not conclude that a life of Jesus could not be written. Instead he proceeded to his own delineation of Jesus, seeking resolutely to let him stand in his own time and thought-world, so remote and alien from our own. In Schweitzer's picture, Jesus appears as a man of mysterious, dark fears and forebodings, who comes to grief in the end through his overwhelming preoccupation with the idea of the impending cataclysmic overthrow of world history. That very factor in Jesus' teaching, his conviction and proclamation that the kingdom of God would arrive any minute, which the Liberals dismissed as "dogmatic," unhistorical, and unimportant, Schweitzer dramatized as the genuinely historical factor of Jesus' ministry. In this Schweitzer was not alone. Some years earlier, in a slim volume entitled *Die Predigt Jesu vom Reiche Gottes* (The Preaching of Jesus on the Kingdom of God), Johannes Weiss had tried to show that the heart of Jesus' message was that *God* will suddenly put an end to the world and history and will bring in a new world in the very near future. The view of Weiss ran counter to the prevailing understanding of the Liberals associated with the theology of Albrecht Ritschl, namely that the kingdom of God in the Gospels should be interpreted as the final goal to be realized by moral and social endeavor on the part of men. The extent to which cultural trends prevalent in the Victorian era—optimism, utopianism, and evolutionism—exerted any direct influence on the course of biblical studies is not easy to assess, and possibly we should not overestimate it. However, the familiar Liberal depiction of Jesus as the Ideal Man or Teacher summoning the righteous in his own and every age to play their part in the ever-expanding kingdom of God on earth certainly corresponded very well to the confident and super-optimistic mood of the time.

Now the kingdom of God in Jesus' teaching, as Weiss understood it, had nothing to do with a paradise on earth constructed gradually by human effort. Since, according to Weiss, Jesus' idea of the kingdom of God was entirely transcendental and belonged so completely to his own place and time, Jesus could not be used, as the Liberals used him, to endorse even their own best social and political dreams and programs, nor indeed their own aesthetic tastes and ethical aspirations.

Weiss and Schweitzer had dealt a devastating blow at the old quest. Even so it died very hard, for through most of the present century, at least in the English-speaking world, a steady flow of Lives of Jesus, which show little advance on what was written in the nineteenth century, continued to find its way into the bookshops. Nevertheless, on the Continent, the Jesus depicted by Weiss and more so by Schweitzer really signaled the demise of the liberal era. From other quarters also the winds of change were blowing toward the turn of the century. The German pietist theologian, Martin Kähler, maintained that the Gospels were first and foremost documents of the Church's faith in Christ. They were never intended to be read, and must not be read, as biographical memoirs of the man Jesus. Rather were they Church proclamations of the crucified and risen Christ. Then again, the historical reliability of Mark was gravely impugned by William Wrede. Critical scholarship had come to accept as more or less axiomatic that Mark's Gospel was not only the first to be written but also offered a substantially accurate record of Jesus' life in regard to the outward course of events or the inward development of his own consciousness. Wrede now argued that, far from being biographically conceived, Mark's account of Jesus was determined by dogmatic or doctrinal considerations belonging to the theology of the early Church.

The genuineness of the Gospels as history was thus seriously called in question. In all this we see the early signs of the coming eclipse of the historical Jesus that was to endure from the 1920s into the 1950s under the impact of the dialectical theology of Karl Barth and Rudolf Bultmann, who initially had this in common with each other that they both reacted rather vehemently against nineteenth-century Liberalism, but who latterly followed each his own quite different theological course. Very shortly after the First World War Bultmann became the leading exponent of a new method of analyzing the Gospel materials. This new development in Gospel study is commonly called Form-criticism, since its primary aim is to sift out and investigate the many different types of stories and sayings of Jesus according to their own particular *form,* content, style, and structure.

Form-criticism as practised not only by Bultmann but also notably by Martin Dibelius achieved two fundamental insights. In the so-called twilight period of some thirty years between the death of Jesus and the composition of Mark the traditions about Jesus had been passed on orally; moreover, they had been transmitted initially *in isolated fragments.* The joining together of these separate fragments only took place later when they were given a connected order according to subject matter. On this view, the Gospel stories of Jesus were really so many disconnected units with no chronological relationship to one another. The narrative of Mark could thus be likened to a string of pearls of which the string had been broken. If that were so, all hope of retrieving from the sources anything like a biography of Jesus was surely gone.

The second insight of Form-criticism had to do with individual units of the tradition of Jesus' words and deeds. Investigation of the *form* of individual texts revealed that the particular shape each had taken went hand in hand with a particular function or need in the life of the early Christian community. In other words, the various interests of the community in mission, teaching, worship, and ecclesiastical organization greatly influenced the formation and transformation of the tradition of Jesus. So the Gospels are a mirror of the collective existence or consciousness of the first Christian congregations. They contain hardly a single trace of the actual history of Jesus.

The Gospels being what they are, the quest of the historical Jesus is impossible. So concluded Bultmann as leading Form-critic. On the other hand, as theologian, he was convinced that the historical Jesus is in any case of small significance for Christian faith and theology. Faith is connected with the crucified and risen Christ preached by the Church. To fall back upon the reconstruction of factual data from the life of Jesus is to seek worldly props and proofs for faith, and so to surrender the possibility of true faith which must live not out of worldly facts but out of the hiddenness of God.

Bultmann's contribution to theological thought is of course far richer and more diverse than is represented here. Our aim has been merely to show in broadest outline why the decline of interest in the historical Jesus in the 1920-50 era should be associated principally with Bultmann's name. Had Bultmann gone too far in denigrating the importance of the historical Jesus? A number of his own students eventually thought so. They felt he was in danger of reducing Christ to a mythical figure divorced entirely from historical reality. So in the early 1950s they began to advocate both the possibility and permissibility of a "new quest" of the historical Jesus. The upshot has been a considerable resurgence of interest in the history of Jesus during the last decade and more.

What is new in the "new quest"? How does it differ from the old liberal quest of the nineteenth century? These are matters of great controversy. But gone now, to be sure, is the former confidence about reconstructing "what actually happened" in the life of Jesus. A biography is altogether out of the question. Since every single word or story of Jesus in the Gospels is interfused with the confession of the believing congregation, the search for the bare facts of history is extremely difficult. But with the "new seekers" after Jesus, the center of interest in any case has been shifted from the outward course of events to the inward side of things. Jesus' aim, his intention, his purpose, which constitute the ground of his existence, these are the proper subjects of enquiry. The words of Jesus (and to a much lesser extent the deeds), which can be judged to be authentic, provide us with some clues from which to read off the meaning of his existence. The "new quest," therefore, concentrates chiefly on the preaching and teaching of Jesus, and gives the most prominent place of all to his proclamation of the coming kingdom of God.

Interesting though this development is, it has hardly been able to get off the ground because of its preoccupation with problems of legitimacy and method. It has in fact been rather barren of positive results, with the possible exception of the one full-scale work on Jesus to come from the Bultmann group, Günther Bornkamm's *Jesus of Nazareth*.[12] The book is in no sense a *life* of Jesus. Rather the author's main concern is to establish the continuity between the Jesus of history and the Christ of the Church's faith and preach-

[12] G. Bornkamm, *Jesus of Nazareth*, trans. Irene and Fraser McLuskey (New York, 1960).

ing, to show what there was in the words (and deeds) of Jesus that could have led the Church after his death to bring Jesus and God together in her confessions of faith. In Bornkamm's pages, brilliant as they often are, the theologian's view of the Christ of the Church and the historian's view of the man Jesus often shade into each other: we cannot be quite sure whether we are standing on firm historical or slippery theological ground. Whether in fact the "new quest" has enabled us to grasp the historical Jesus any better than before is open to debate.

In the foregoing sketch of the course of Jesus-research in the last two centuries, we have noted the vigor of the life of Jesus movement of the nineteenth century, its eventual demise before the onslaught of Form-criticism and the dialectical theology, and finally the recent resurgence of interest in the historical Jesus in the "new quest." It should not be supposed, however, that the same single track of development has been neatly followed everywhere in the world. Outside of Germany, in England and America, for instance, there has been continuing opposition to the skepticism of Form-criticism, and a steady emphasis on the important role played by eyewitnesses of Jesus' ministry in the transmission of the tradition, the activity of eyewitnesses being taken (mistakenly?) as a guarantee of the historical trustworthiness of the Gospels. And lately Scandinavian scholars have contended that Form-criticism has all along worked with completely erroneous historical presuppositions. The traditions of Jesus' words and deeds did not in fact circulate in the first Christian congregations in the free and volatile fashion associated with *folklore*. Rather were they confined within a fixed channel. The apostles formed a sort of college in Jerusalem after the model of the Jewish rabbinical schools. In their teaching in Jerusalem they depended on those words and acts of Jesus that had been passed on to them. And Jesus himself, like the Jewish teachers of his day "must have made his disciples learn certain sayings by heart; if he taught, he must have required his disciples to memorize." [13] As loyal students they would not have attempted to alter Jesus' teachings. Accordingly what has eventually passed into the written Gospels is the actual teaching of Jesus in materially unchanged form.

The Scandinavian view of the tradition we have just outlined

[13] B. Gerhardsson, *Memory and Manuscript: Oral Tradition and Written Transmission in Rabbinic Judaism and Early Christianity,* trans. E. J. Sharpe (Lund and Copenhagen, 1961), p. 13.

has not met with much favor. In fact, although the significance of Jesus' having couched some at least of his teaching in easily memorized form should certainly not be minimized, the view has some real weaknesses. It fails to explain why, if the words of Jesus were handed on in such a deterministic or mechanistic fashion, the Gospels should contain variant reports of single sayings of Jesus. Further while the Twelve unquestionably figured largely in the emergence of Christianity, there is hardly sufficient evidence that they made up a kind of central panel on doctrine intent on transmitting Jesus' teachings as a securely preserved "Holy Word." The process of transmission culminating in the Gospels is different from that operative in the mother faith. Judaism always distinguishes between its Mishnah, its authoritative "Holy Word" and its Talmud, its *gemara* or comment on the "Holy Word." But in the Gospels no distinction is drawn between *ipsissima verba* of Jesus and the materials which arose from the use of his words in the Christian community and became fused with them. No doubt what counted most for primitive Christianity was not a fixed code of the sacred words of the Lord, but the person of Jesus Christ himself.[14] Through their experience of the continuing presence of Jesus Christ after the resurrection, the early congregations became marked by "enthusiasm" in the best sense the word has in the history of religions. The life they lived was lived under the inspiration of the Spirit, and since the Spirit spelled freedom for them, most likely their "enthusiasm" tended far less toward the safe preservation of a static "Holy Word" than toward flexibility and the readiness to adapt the tradition in the face of ever-changing needs and challenges.

We may fairly say that so far no branch of criticism has provided us with any sure or universally acceptable formula for sifting out the authentic historical from the theological or evangelical element in the Gospels. The field of Jesus-research has been all through the scene of a rather painful conflict of conservative and radical tendencies, of confidence in the historical trustworthiness of the Gospels and extreme doubt. But perhaps for too long too many have expected too much from these documents. We have imagined that they should place in our grasp the figure of Jesus "as he really was in himself" as an isolated and idealized individual. But to wish

[14] See W. D. Davies, *The Setting of the Sermon on the Mount* (Cambridge, 1964), pp. 464ff.

for so much is to wish Jesus out of the historical process, for history has a lot to do with impact and reaction, impression and response, relationship and encounter between person and person. Insofar as the Gospels do not separate Jesus from the concrete world in which he lived, but show him as a real man in contact with real men, they simply will not yield to our facile and unjustifiable modernization whereby we hope to extract from them the "timeless essence" of his life in capsule form and in one easy lesson, so to speak.

Such historical information as the Gospel tradition conveys is conveyed not in a clear-cut, single picture of Jesus, but in a series of impressions he made on other people. Jesus of course, long after his death and resurrection, continued to impress believers in the Church in different ways. But properly the historian seeks to catch the first level of impressions that Jesus made on various groups of people in Judaea and Galilee during his ministry.

Lately, by means of what is known as redaction-criticism, we have been learning a good deal more about the theological aims and motives of each Evangelist from the manner in which he has combined the traditions that have come to him into the overall framework or pattern of his Gospel. Here is promise for the future, since the more we know of the culminating stage of the formation of each Gospel and the reasons why it has been given the shape it has, the better position we should be in to focus upon the earliest stage of impressions the historical Jesus had on his contemporaries. But the limits imposed on us should be frankly recognized—the most we may look for by way of history in the Gospel tradition is not all that was in Jesus "as he was in himself," but the varying responses he evoked from the folk he met through the different impressions he made on them.

This Introduction has so far ranged over a fairly wide area. Yet we have said practically nothing directly about the life of Jesus of Nazareth. There is a very good reason why this should be so. The gateway to the story of Jesus is in the first place the story of the search for his life and history since the Age of the Enlightenment. If Jesus himself had written even one "Gospel," it would have greatly simplified the historian's task and restricted the possibilities. Obviously it is the scantiness of the materials on Jesus and the complex character of the sources mentioned at the outset that have enabled the writing of so many books about him, expressing countless divergent opinions, and indulging frequently in speculative and fanciful "reconstructions." Today, therefore, nobody should imagine that the search for the historical Jesus can be brought at last to a new and violent solution by one sharp thrust on the Gordian knot. "Without the process of criticism and counter-criticism there is no knowledge of historical truth in this field or in any other." [15] Honest study of the life of Jesus demands concentrated effort of the mind to understand this process of criticism. But so long as a very large sector of mankind believes that something of decisive importance happened in Palestine two thousand years ago, who is to say the effort will not be worthwhile?

It happened in Palestine! Jesus' person and history belong to a particular religious, social, political, and cultural background. Precisely because of the dearth of materials shedding light on Jesus personally and directly, background studies in his case assume an even greater importance than usual. Hence we have to try to form a picture of his period and environment.

The chronology of Jesus' ministry is an intricate problem. The Gospels offer very few specific notices of dates. Exceptional is Luke's attempt at a precise dating in the beginning of his Gospel: "Now in the fifteenth year of the reign of Tiberius Caesar, Pontius Pilate being governor of Judaea, and Herod being tetrarch of Galilee, and his brother Philip tetrarch of Iturea and of the region of Trachonitis, and Lysanias the tetrarch of Abilene, Annas and Caiaphas being the high priests, the word of God came unto John the son of Zacharias in the wilderness." (Luke 3:1-2). Luke also mentions that Jesus was about thirty years old at the moment he began his ministry (Luke 3:23). From these and other indications we may gather that Jesus was born shortly before the death of Herod the Great in 4 B.C. and died possibly during the Passover of A.D. 28.

That he was born and reared a Jew is scarcely in doubt—despite the fact that his homeland of Galilee (the name denotes "circle of Gentiles") was subject to the strongest Gentile influences and numbered in its population only a small Jewish minority, and despite recurrent efforts to prove his Aryan origin (e.g. by Houston St. Chamberlain, *Foundations of the Nineteenth Century,* trans. John Lees, I [1910], 200ff.). By the time of Jesus the Jewish nation possessed barely a vestige of political power. Ever since the return from the Babylonian exile (586-538 B.C.), Judaea was a land to be coveted by rival imperialisms. Because of its strategic boundary

[15] Bornkamm, *op. cit.,* p. 10.

situation it had been subjected to endless pressures from ambitious world powers, from the Persians to Alexander the Great and his conquests, from the Ptolemies of Egypt to the Greeks of the Seleucid empire in Syria, from the erstwhile intervention of the Parthians to the final dominion of Rome. Yet no political, social or economic disaster could ever shake this small nation loose from the foundations of its existence. The true foundation of its life was the God its people worshipped, and to whose gracious will they traced their origin. Their God bore no resemblance whatever to an Oriental despot, but was for them the Holy One who desired justice and mercy and punished sin, and who loved his own as a father loves his first-born son. Covenant loyalty to this "other" God marked the Jews off from their pagan neighbors and constituted them a peculiar people. Again and again they stubbornly resisted the influence of foreign cultures so that to the outsider they seemed strangely intransigent and backward.

The supreme crisis and clash of Judaism with an external culture took place in the first half of the second century B.C. Exposed to Greek influence from the time of Alexander the Great and before, a minority of the Jewish aristocracy and the priestly leaders in Jerusalem had shown some openness to Greek ways of life. Possibly misguided as to the strength of the people's affection for Greek culture, the Syrian king, Antiochus IV Epiphanes (175-163 B.C.) fancied he could set up a Greek *polis* in Jerusalem. In 168 B.C. he entered the city and later erected there by way of retaliation on opponents a pagan altar to Zeus. Jewish cultic practices were proscribed and heathen rites substituted for them. Antiochus was motivated not by zeal for religious reform but by political aspirations. He saw the advantages to be gained from controlling the Jews as a biddable subject people. But the "desolating sacrilege" he had erected in the Temple branded him in the eyes of the Jewish Community as a *religious* persecutor and, to that extent, made an uprising on their part inevitable.

So Antiochus' actions precipitated the revolutionary struggle of the Maccabees for release from foreign oppression. The gallantry of Judas Maccabaeus and his brothers, and the epic courage of the martyred soldiers of the faith who followed them have been extolled in Jewish tradition. Judas in fact is credited with having restored full religious freedom to his people. But in addition, his exploits in guerrilla warfare so widened the boundaries of the nation as to revive memories of the glorious days of David and Solomon. Unhappily the taste of renewed political prestige proved to be a too heady wine. The seeds of corruption of the pristine religious idealism of the Maccabaean movement were sown already when Judas had the high priest made king. Consequently the history of the later successors of the Maccabees degenerated into a history of political intrigue, traitorous dealings with the foreigner, and internecine party strife.

Ironically the final doom of the Jewish nation as a politically independent entity was sealed by ruling men of Jewish blood. Hyrcanus and Aristobulus, the last sons of the Hasmonaean dynasty (Judas Maccabaeus had been a member of the house of Hasmon), were rival claimants for the throne of Judaea when the Roman general Pompey appeared in Damascus in 63 B.C. They requested him to arbitrate in their dispute. Pompey's interference was dearly bought. He seized the opportunity to invest Jerusalem, entered the Holy of Holies in the Temple, and exacted tribute from the Jews. Hyrcanus was installed in the office of ethnarch and high priest, while the bothersome Aristobulus was carried off captive to Rome. From now on the Romans were the real overlords of Palestine. And besides, between the Romans and Hyrcanus and the Jews stood another key figure in the person of Antipater II, governor of Idumaea (an office he had inherited from his father, Antipas or Antipater). As Hyrcanus' minister, Antipater wielded the reins of government in Judaea.

The civil war that broke out between Pompey and Caesar in 49 B.C., so far as it affected the Jews, served mainly to demonstrate Antipater's skill in aligning himself with the winning cause in Rome, a skill that paid off when Caesar confirmed him as procurator of Judaea and offered concessions to the Jewish people. Chaos followed the assassination of Caesar in 44 B.C. and led to the downfall and violent death of Antipater and the rise of his son Herod. Showing no less prowess than his father had done in negotiating with the Romans, Herod secured the friendship of Anthony and Octavian, and on their recommendation the Roman senate voted him king of the land. But it took Herod all of three years to establish in fact the kingdom he now owned by Roman right.

Herod's long reign was marked by violent contradictions. There was on the one hand Herod, unswervingly loyal to Rome, architect-in-chief of the most lavish building projects, on occasion magnanimous toward his Jewish subjects, and on the other hand Herod anything but "great," Oriental tyrant, capable of barbaric cruelty, paranoiac even in the palace. As the favored ally of Rome, Herod was able to indulge in an extensive building program of fortresses, gymnasiums, aqueducts, baths, fountains, colonnades, cities, and temples dedicated to Caesar Augustus. His reconstruction of the temple in Jerusalem and erection of the fort and tower named Antonia in the northwest corner of the temple area helped to give Jerusalem the magnificent appearance it enjoyed in the time of Jesus. But all this style and splendor afforded no pleasure to the Jews. They hated Herod as an Idumaean outsider (bitter enmity between Israel and Edom was traditional). His subservience to Rome and his recognition of the cult of Caesar they grievously resented. Insecure and panicky, Herod only made matters far worse by resorting to drastic purges in his court and wholesale murder in his household riddled with jealousies and plots and counterplots among the women of his harem. The personification in Herod of the Roman dominion over Palestine, the wild and insane last days of his rule, the contempt of the Jewish people for him and everything he stood for all set the political stage for the coming of Jesus.

On the death of Herod, the failure of Jewish overtures to Caesar Augustus to end the Herodian rule was followed by Rome's division of the country among Herod's sons. Archelaus was made governor of Judaea, Samaria and Idumaea; Herod Antipas who was to become the sovereign of John the Baptist and Jesus, tetrarch of Galilee and Peraea; Philip tetrarch of the region east and northeast of the Sea of Galilee. The three small vassal states were short-lived. Judaea was the first to go, when in A.D. 6 Archelaus was deposed and banished by the emperor for his "barbarous and tyrannical" actions. Loosely attached to the Roman province of Syria, Judaea was now to be administered by a Roman procurator, who, with his official residence in Caesarea, was military commander-in-chief of the area and responsible for the levying and collection of taxes through the agency of Jewish tax collectors.

In the succession of procurators, the name which has come down to history is that of Pontius Pilate (A.D. 26-36). Like others of his predecessors, he apparently had a penchant for provoking the Jews. On his first entry into Jerusalem, his military escort sorely wounded Jewish religious susceptibilities by carrying ensigns bearing the emperor's image. Pilate's greatest notoriety of course consists in the fact that it was under him the ministry, arrest, trial, and execution of Jesus occurred.

On the whole, however, even while the Romans could not fully understand the "mystique" of Judaism, they displayed enlightened political wisdom in allowing the Jews a large measure of freedom in the practice of their religion. No more could the Jews understand the Roman masters. They chafed at the bit under the slightest provocation; sporadic acts of sedition flared up. In A.D. 6 insurrection had broken out in Galilee under a certain Judas. Thereafter bands of men called Zealots, aflame with hopes of the overthrow of the Roman yoke and the coming of the Jewish Messiah, lost no opportunity of harassing the Romans by means of violence and inciting their fellow-countrymen to open revolt.

After the death of the last Herodian, Agrippa I, in A.D. 44, movements inspired by the theocratic ideal and passionate Messianic expectations multiplied. These ceaseless minor revolutions ended in the collapse of Jerusalem and its final destruction by the Romans in A.D. 70 and in the extinction of all political independence for the Jewish people. Viewed politically, the history of the Jews from the fervent ideals of the earliest Maccabaean leaders and the grandeurs of the state under them to the fall of Jerusalem presents a melancholy and tragic decline. With the ultimate blow of A.D. 70, "Jewishness" should have died. Instead Judaism has survived that catastrophe until today, as indeed it had survived all previous catastrophes. And if we ask why, the only possible answer lies surely in the unique staying-power of Jewish religious faith and hope.

The pages of the Gospels testify to the variety and fluidity of Jewish religious life in the time of Jesus. A number of distinct parties and tendencies appear, and clearly the most prominent are the Pharisees and Sadducees. At the beginning of the Maccabaean revolt there emerged in support of the rebels a group of loyalists called the Chasidim (Pious Ones), earnestly devoted to the Jewish Law. Only when the Maccabaean struggle for religious liberty gave way to political ambitions and the secularization of the priesthood did these Chasidim withdraw their allegiance. The Pharisees are usually understood to have been the descendants of the Chasidim. Certainly they shared the Chasidim's passion for the Law, and as the name "Pharisee" implies (it is usually thought to be derived from the Hebrew *pārash* and to mean "separated"), they refused to have any truck with the sophisticated aristocratic minority in

Judaism who courted Greek influence or with the "people of the land," the peasant class, who were ignorant of the Law. Their great preoccupation was to establish the Law as the supreme and sole guide to all the duties and decisions and practical actions of daily life. And in the institution of the synagogue they had a ready-made instrument for trying to accomplish this. With the synagogue as center, and with the aid of the scribes who were members of the Pharisee movement, they studied the Law of Moses assiduously and sought to apply the ancient commandments afresh to the changing conditions of their own day. Progressives and innovators, they did not confine themselves to the written Law of Moses, but appealed also to an oral tradition which they believed to be of no less venerable antiquity and authority than the written Scripture itself. The expositions of Scripture developed by them were construed as the continuation and adaptation of that long-standing oral tradition, designed to meet new situations and needs in Jewish society. Not least, perhaps, because it attempted to bring the ancient Law up to date and to say something relevant to the "modern man," Pharisaism had a widespread popular following among the Jews. At its best, to be sure, Pharisaism was not lacking in the dynamic of genuine religious experience; it knew the joy of obedience to the will of the Lord: it knew the difference between the spirit and the letter of the Law. But at its worst, by reason of its desire to legislate for every minutest detail of daily living, Pharisaism was inclined to become an elaborate casuistry and a restrictive legalism. The question of Sabbath observance, as we gather from the rabbinic literature, was endlessly debated. Does rescuing an animal from a well into which it has fallen constitute a breach of the Sabbath rest? Does the lifting of a chair on the Sabbath mean the command about not carrying burdens has been broken? Can one eat an egg laid on the Sabbath? The Gospels reflect a serious clash between Jesus and his understanding of the will of God and the Pharisees and their brand of legalistic piety.

By contrast with the Pharisees, the Sadducees were the conservative party. Their origins are obscure, their structure and outlook toward the time of Jesus fairly clear to us. Refusing to accept as binding anything save the *written* Law of Moses, unlike the liberalizing Pharisees, the relatively small group of the Sadducees was drawn mainly from the priestly ruling caste, who had their homes in and around Jerusalem and were in control of the temple there. Intent on protecting their vested interests, they tended to submit readily to whatever outside regime happened to exercise power in Judaea and to welcome external pagan cultural influences. Together with the Pharisees and the leading laymen of the people called the "elders," the Sadducees, or their representatives, made up the supreme court of Judaism in Jerusalem, the Sanhedrin. In the arrest and trial of Jesus, through their high priest who acted as chairman of the Sanhedrin, the Sadducees played a leading role (Mark 11:27; 14:1,53; 15:1). In the light of Jesus' interference in the management of the temple (Mark 11:15-18), the animosity of the Sadducees against him is understandable.

While the Pharisee-Sadducee parties helped largely to shape the Judaism Jesus knew, of course not every Jew in his day was inevitably either a Pharisee or a Sadducee. The situation was much more complex. For one thing, the rivalry between Jews and the schismatic Samaritans of the north of Palestine had become greatly intensified. Although the temple the Samaritans had built on Mount Gerizim as a competitor to the Jerusalem temple had long since been destroyed (128 B.C.), they had their own Holy Scripture, their own special form of expectation of the Messiah, and followed their own religious customs and observances. They were despised by the Jews as religiously unclean because of their intermarriage with foreigners (see the parable of the Good Samaritan in Luke 10:30-37).

Again, and more significantly, there were the splinter groups of Essenes who broke away from the main line of Jewish public life in order to form the true essential priestly Judaism. Hitherto we knew of the Essenes and their main characteristics from the Jewish writers, Philo and Josephus. But since the discovery of the Dead Sea Scrolls in 1947, copious evidence has come to light of the existence of a rigorous Essene-like community that had its main headquarters near the northwest shore of the Dead Sea. The sect of the Covenanters of Qumrân (a subject touched on previously) was a withdrawal or separatist movement, which in its beginnings during the days of the Maccabaean revolt had affinities with the Chasidim and with incipient Pharisaism. Quite probably dissatisfaction with the growing secularism of the priestly ruling class and with the low moral pitch of run-of-the-mill Judaism led to their retreat into the seclusion of the wilderness. At any rate the separated "Congregation of the Covenant" certainly saw themselves as the true Israel, the "children of light," the elect group who alone were fit and ready for the impending arrival of the judgment of God.

Initiation into the sect involved severe tests over a stern period of probation. Community life was rigidly disciplined and strictly organized. Meticulous attention was paid to matters of ritual cleanliness; the practice of asceticism was the order of the day; members shared regularly in sacramental meals. The whole life of the community had a strong priestly flavor, one interesting illustration of which is the fact that they were expecting the coming not only of a kingly Messiah of the house of David and of a figure of the End time called "The Prophet," but also of a *priestly Messiah of the house of Aaron.*

Under the inspiration of their unidentified leader and founder, the Righteous Teacher, they were completely dedicated to perfect obedience to the Law in its entirety. Strong on law and order, they were by no means wanting either in ardor. Documents produced by them like *The War of the Children of Light and the Children of Darkness* show how enthusiastically they believed themselves to be engaged in the conflict with evil that was shortly leading up to the vindication of the "children of light" in the new age of God. The Qumrân group were, moreover, the custodians of numerous other writings of a like nature, penned outside the sect and belonging to that peculiar literary genre termed apocalyptic. In the grim days of the Maccabaean revolt the hope that had previously been nurtured in Israel of the coming restoration of the nation through the advent of a Messiah of David's line no longer seemed adequate by itself to match the moment. Growing pessimism was in the air. History appeared to have no purpose or goal, not in the present world. The upshot of this somber mood was a crop of apocalyptic works, the classic model of which is the Book of Daniel. Into such works crept the influence of Babylonian and Persian mythological beliefs in angels and demons. Apocalyptic purported to convey in visions, couched in cryptic language and bizarre imagery, the secret contours of the Last Days. Jewish expectations of the coming great future were extended in scope and given a transcendent or cosmic dimension. A new type of hoped-for Messianic figure made his appearance in the concept of the heavenly "Man" of Daniel 7:13, who would come on the clouds in judgment and gather the elect into a holy people, or the mysterious "son of man" of I Enoch and IV Ezra.

For long enough it used to be supposed that the overwhelming interest of Judaism around the time of Jesus was the Law and all matters pertaining thereto. Apocalyptic was merely peripheral to "normative Judaism," the legal Judaism of Pharisaism and the rabbinic schools. Was that so "normative" after all? In view of Qumrân and our increased knowledge of contemporary Judaism, we have had to revise our former estimate. We now see more clearly that the apocalyptic outlook and mode of thought infiltrated nearly all sectors of Judaism, and that the Pharisees themselves were by no means immune. The domain of the Law certainly, but no less the strange world of apocalyptic, makes up the landscape against which alone the work and words of Jesus can be understood.

Although neither the Essenes in general nor the Essene-like congregation of Qumrân in particular are mentioned in the New Testament, it is now generally agreed that clear lines of connection can be traced between the primitive Christian communities and the Qumrân sect. Among other things, both had baptismal rites; both completed the process of initiation with participation in sacred meals; both shared common liturgical practices; both observed the principle of a community of goods; both took an apparently critical attitude toward the service of the Jerusalem temple and of sacrifice. But what of a possible relationship of John the Baptist or Jesus himself with the Qumrân community?

There is no evidence of any direct contact between John or Jesus and Qumrân. The differences between these two and Qumrân are more noteworthy than the similarities. John admitted Jews to baptism without summoning them to withdraw from the world into a separatist or exclusivist community like Qumrân. Jesus had none of the priestly or ascetic marks of the sect, and his compassionate concern for all the people as well as his freedom in eating with tax collectors and sinners and in criticizing the laws of the Sabbath or of purification distinguish him clearly from the Qumrân group. Nevertheless it cannot be denied that in their most crucial views John and Jesus both bear points of resemblance to the sectarians. Like them, the Baptist expected and proclaimed the near arrival of the kingdom of God and called for a movement of repentance in the face of it. Like them, Jesus also was urgently awaiting the End time; he shared their belief in the activity of "The Prophet" at the close of history, since he evidently thought of John the Baptist as Elijah returned (See Malachi 4:5 and Mark 9:13).

Many on the Christian side customarily take offense at any hint that Jesus might not have been absolutely original. As if it were not folly to imagine that his teaching should represent a complete break with the wisdom of the ages! But in particular it has to be pointed out here that the great question with Qumrân or with the Church, founded by the life, death, and resurrection of Jesus, was not how "new" or *avant garde* each could be in theology and religion. The great question was which group could most properly be understood as the inheritor of the promises God had made long ago to Israel and as the chosen agent of God to prepare for the final coming of his kingdom. Not for nothing did the primitive Church seek first of all to substantiate the "newness" of Jesus by having recourse to the old, by turning to the Old Testament to find texts to illustrate and illumine his life and work, and above all to demonstrate his Messiahship.[16]

The evidence from Qumrân has certainly filled out our knowledge of contemporary Judaism, especially the variety and vitality of Messianic hopes prevalent in Jesus' day. While the Pharisees and Qumrân community both entertained their own Messianic expectations, neither body had any wish to interfere actively in politics. It was left to others to turn the Messianic hopes into a political program. The avowed aim of the party of the Zealots was to throw off the burden of Roman taxation by the use of armed force. The Zealot movement spawned a series of abortive Messianic uprisings, in which now one "prophet" now another claimed to be Messiah and gathered round him a rebel band to lead against the Romans. With good cause the Romans regarded all these insurrections as a distinct threat to their security and proceeded to stamp them out forthwith. Even where Messianic expectations were simply cherished by Jews who awaited a miracle of God without in any wise resorting to political action, the Romans were justifiably suspicious.

Under all these troubled circumstances of the age, the Roman condemnation and execution of Jesus is more readily understood. Not that Jesus was anything like the revolutionary Messianic "prophets" mentioned above—only real distortion of the Gospel evidence can make him so. The only prophet with whom Jesus was closely associated was John the Baptist. And John was an open-air preacher of the desert, not a political fanatic.

The ministry of John the Baptist provided the immediate point

[16] See K. Stendahl, ed., *The Scrolls and Christian Origins* (New York, 1957).

of departure for the ministry of Jesus. The significance of John the Baptist for the early Church is reflected in the fact that only Jesus, Peter, and Paul are mentioned more often in the New Testament than he is. Precisely because the Gospel stories about John are told from the standpoint of his significance for the early Church, they have been shaped and colored by the community's beliefs. Accordingly, in the Gospels we can see the process whereby John's own individual genius and his work in its own right are subordinated to the climactic role of Jesus as the Messiah. The process culminates in the Fourth Gospel where John renounces all claims for himself and becomes simply the witness to Jesus' Messiahship, indeed to the Christian message in its entirety (John 1:36 and 3:25-36). Possibly the author of the Fourth Gospel felt he had to emphasize the inferiority of John the Baptist because, in the context where he lived, he was aware of the influence of a Baptist sect which acknowledged John as its founder and leader. Possibly also the community of the Mandaeans, which emerged later and which survives to this day, was descended from these followers of the Baptist.

However, the accounts of the Baptist in the Gospels do contain a sufficient residue of history to enable us to gather something of his character and activity. As we have noted already, he appeared in the wilderness by the Jordan river in the guise of a prophet. His garb of camel skin and leather girdle, and his diet of locusts and wild honey are reminiscent of Elijah. He proclaimed to all that God's judgment was coming very shortly, and on the ground of his conviction he summoned his people to repentance. "You brood of vipers! Who warned you to flee from the wrath to come? Bear fruit that befits repentance, and do not presume to say to yourselves, We have Abraham as our father; for I tell you, God is able from these stones to raise up children to Abraham. Even now the axe is laid to the root of the trees; every tree therefore that does not bear good fruit is cut down and thrown into the fire." (Matthew 3:7-10). Like John, the Old Testament prophets had prophesied the coming judgment of God. But with John the "even now" has sounded; the bell is tolling already the arrival of God's kingdom; the situation is extremely urgent; there is no time to lose. The Jewish people can now no longer lean back on the merits of their forefathers. They must themselves repent now and be baptized forthwith. So in ritual preparation for the coming rule of God, John baptized in the Jordan those who came to him. Among those who came was

Jesus. For the Baptist Jesus had apparently the highest respect (see Matthew 11:7-14; Luke 7:24-30). In fact Jesus came to look upon him as the returned Elijah who was to prepare the people of God for the advent of the Messiah (Mark 9:9-13; Matthew 17:9-13).

The mission of John and the mission of Jesus are closely interwoven. But Jesus could not become a follower of the Baptist. He had his own message to proclaim and his own destiny to fulfill. And whereas John had heralded the future coming of God's kingdom, Jesus heralds its presence already in and through his own words and deeds.

PART ONE

HISTORICAL FEATURES OF JESUS' MINISTRY AND MESSAGE

1

Focus on the Historical Facts

Jesus himself wrote nothing. The Gospels, almost our only sources for his life, are certainly not primarily biographical in plan or intention. To extract what we can of the history of Jesus from the documents of the believing Church is, therefore, no easy task. Nevertheless we should not surrender too easily to excessive skepticism. The Gospels do narrate. *They do point us to a historical figure. The thirty years or so that elapsed between the death of Jesus and the writing of the earliest Gospel of Mark around* A.D. *65 is after all a relatively short time. Not long enough, to be sure, for the traditions of Jesus' words and deeds to have been shaped and reshaped by the "collective consciousness" of the community in a fashion so uncontrolled that all trace of his history is lost! Besides, eyewitnesses of his ministry are involved in handing down these same traditions. And as to the words of Jesus at least, there is reason to think that he often couched them in a form that could be easily memorized by his disciples and passed on accurately.*

Supposing that actual historical fact can be recovered from the Gospels, the question is how much. Here the Gospel criticism of the last century and more has been for us a school of learning and discipline. We should know now to avoid the romantic expansions of Jesus' career that are perhaps suited to children's lessons but unjustified by the texts. We should shun sentimental incursions into the soul of Jesus, which the texts do not disclose. We should try not to fill out from our own imagination, in the interest of a more spellbinding tale, what the texts are saying.

Criticism has in fact gradually inflicted on us a painful diminution of our stock of knowledge of the historical Jesus.

The procedure we adopt here is to put the last stage first, to start with the assured historical minimum that criticism has left us. Günther Bornkamm's recent work on Jesus of Nazareth is the outcome of advanced critical research. The book includes a chapter on the "indisputably historical traits" of Jesus' life. The chapter is brief; not much "indisputable history" is included, hardly enough, no doubt, to satisfy many observers of Jesus. Yet the minimal historical picture here presented should serve as a useful touchstone for evaluating the several views of Jesus presented later in these pages.

In the following extract from Bornkamm, the reader should note what is omitted:

1. Hardly a thing is said about the birth, infancy, or early years of Jesus. The birth and infancy stories of Matthew and Luke are largely legendary in character and do not contribute to a history of Jesus.

2. No attempt is made to reconstruct what Catholic theologians call the "hidden life" of Jesus, the years of preparation through his Galilean childhood and youth. About these years the Gospels leave us completely in the dark. Only the last part of Jesus' life, his public ministry, is opened to our view in the Gospels. And the very duration of that ministry we do not even know for certain, just over three years if we follow John, around a year if we follow the other Gospels.

3. There is no playing of the "personality game" with the Jesus of the Gospels. No facing him with those slightly absurd questions beloved of modern educational employment agencies. Has he leadership qualities? A developed sense of responsibility? Is he a good mixer? Does he cooperate well with both equals and seniors? Has he a sense of humor? The Gospels are in fact simply not interested in Jesus' personality in anything like that sense.

4. The question of the "self-consciousness" of Jesus is kept in the background. Did he think of himself as Messiah? As Son of Man? As Son of God? Did he go up to Jerusalem at last with specific intent to die, constrained by the ideal of the Suffering Servant of Israel prophesied of old by Isaiah? On these matters the Gospels give hints, no more. They yield no conclusive answers.

5. No estimate is offered of the part played by Jesus in the history of the Jewish people, of the Roman empire, or the

wider conflicts of world politics. The Gospels themselves indeed offer no such estimate. Rather they are concerned with Jesus' ministry as the "End" of all history.

Now, on the positive side, careful attention should be paid to what is included and emphasized in Bornkamm's historical outline:

1. Jesus' baptism by John and his connection with the movement of the Baptist is of the utmost importance.

2. Most important of all as the chief clue to an understanding of Jesus' being is his message. He is a prophet of the coming Kingdom of God, and more than a prophet, for he feels no need to establish his credentials or justify his message like the Old Testament prophets. Jesus is also a teacher, and as a teacher he is like a Jewish rabbi, and yet more than a rabbi—unlike the typical rabbi he wanders around the countryside and, above all, allows his words always to carry their own authority, an authority underived from the sacred Scripture of Israel. The supreme and unprecedented authority of his speech is reflected by questions like these in the Gospels: What is this—a new teaching? Whence did this fellow get this wisdom? Why does he speak this way? How has this man known without having studied?

GÜNTHER BORNKAMM: "THE ROUGH OUTLINES OF JESUS' PERSON AND HISTORY" [1]

The nature of the sources does not permit us to paint a biographical picture of the life of Jesus against the background of the history of his people and his age. Nevertheless, what these sources do yield as regards the historical facts concerning the personality and career of Jesus is not negligible, and demands careful attention. We shall, therefore, try first of all to compile the main historically indisputable traits, and to present the rough outlines of Jesus' person and history. In doing this, we must, of course, desist from rash combinations of the biographical data and must use the greatest critical caution in order to be able really to focus those facts which are prior to any pious interpretation and which manifest themselves as undistorted and primary.

[1] From G. Bornkamm, *Jesus of Nazareth,* trans. Irene and Fraser McLuskey with J. M. Robinson (New York: Harper & Row, Publishers, 1960), pp. 52-55. Reprinted by permission of the publisher.

The childhood and adolescence of Jesus are obscure for us from the historical point of view. The birth narratives in Matthew and Luke, which differ from one another not inconsiderably, are too much overgrown by legends and by Jewish as well as Christian messianic conceptions to be used for historical assertions. The importance and meaning of these texts lie in a different area. The home of Jesus is the semi-pagan, despised Galilee. His native town is Nazareth. His family certainly belonged to the Jewish part of the population which, since the times of the Maccabees, had reattached themselves to the temple cult in Jerusalem and the legal practices of Judaism. Only a criticism blinded by racial ideologies could deny the Jewish origin of Jesus. Jesus' father was a carpenter, and possibly he himself was too. We know the names of his parents, Joseph and Mary, and those of his brothers, James, Joses, Judas and Simon (Mk. vi. 3). His brothers—as well as his mother—were originally unbelievers (Mk. iii. 21, 31; Jn. vii. 5), but later belonged to the Church and to its missionaries (Acts i. 14; I Cor. ix. 5). The tradition occasionally also mentions Jesus' sisters (Mk. vi. 3; Mt. xiii. 56). Jesus' mother tongue is the Aramaic of Galilee, the same dialect by which the servants of the high priest recognise Peter when he denies his Master in Jerusalem (Mt. xxvi. 73). Hebrew was at that time no longer a spoken language, but rather only the language of religion and of scholars (somewhat comparable to the ecclesiastical Slavonic of the Orthodox Church). As a Jewish rabbi he must have been able to understand the ancient language of the Bible. On the other hand, we do not know to what extent he and his disciples knew Greek, widely used in administration and commerce. At any rate we find in Jesus no trace of the influence of Greek philosophy or of the Greek manner of living, just as nothing is known of activity on his part in the Hellenistic towns of the country. Rather we hear of his activity in the smaller hamlets and villages—Bethsaida, Chorazin, Capernaum—in the hill country and round the Sea of Galilee.

According to an isolated note in Luke, Jesus' public ministry begins, following the work of John the Baptist, at about his thirtieth year (Lk. iii. 23). His own baptism by John is one of the most certainly verified occurrences of his life. Tradition, however, has altogether transformed the story into a testimony to the Christ, so that we cannot gather from it what baptism meant for Jesus himself, for his decisions and for his inner development. But that this event was of far-reaching importance nobody will deny. It is all the more important that Jesus, without ever questioning the mission and the authority of the Baptist, nevertheless does not continue the work of the Baptist and his followers in the Jordan valley, but starts his own work in Galilee—like John, as a prophet of the coming kingdom of God. The instrument of his activity, however, is no longer baptism, but his spoken word and helping hand. We can no longer say with certainty how long Jesus' activity lasted. The first three Gospels create the impression that it lasted but a year. But they do not give a reliable chronology. We learn a great deal about his preaching, the conflict with his opponents, his healing and the additional help he granted the suffering, and the powerful influence which went forth from him. The people flock to him. Disciples follow him, but his enemies also arise and increase. All this will have to occupy us later. Here we are only concerned with the rough outlines of his life and his work. The last decisive turning point in his life is the resolution to go to Jerusalem with his disciples in order to confront the people there with his message in face of the coming kingdom of God. At the end of this road is his death on the cross. These meagre, indisputable facts comprise a very great deal. There is little enough in this enumeration, and yet it contains most important information about the life story of Jesus and its stages.

GÜNTHER BORNKAMM: "ENCOUNTER WITH JESUS" [2]

Much remains hidden in the obscurity of history. Tradition does not yield a logical and detailed account of the course of Jesus' life. Nevertheless, the Gospels furnish much more material as regards the outlines of his historical person seen in the setting of his own world. We shall, therefore, recall the picture of that world in which he appeared.

As we saw, time and history, the past and the future, determine in a unique way the thought, experience and hopes of the Jewish people. This people finds its God and itself in the past, in which its life and character were given to it; and in the future, in which its life and its character are to be restored to it. It knows no other security, even in a present which reveals nothing of this certainty and seems to mock this people's claim. It knows its sole task as that of guarding faithfully this past and this future. Thus the world in

[2] G. Bornkamm, *op. cit.*, pp. 55-59. Reprinted by permission of the publisher.

which Jesus appears is a world between past and future; it is so strongly identified with the one and with the other that, according to the Jewish faith, the immediate present is practically non-existent. The whole of life is caught in a network of sacred traditions. Everyone has his place within a structure determined and ordered by the law and promise of God. Whoever lives up to this divine system can claim eternal salvation; whoever does not is rejected. All time is time between, and as such it is a time of stewardship, founded in God's decisions of the past and looking forward to God's decisions in the future, which mean salvation or destruction for each one. We can now understand the strange picture presented by the historical milieu in which Jesus lived. It is comparable to a soil hardened and barren through its age-long history and tradition, yet a volcanic, eruptive ground, out of whose cracks and crevices breaks forth again and again the fire of a burning expectation. However, both, torpidity and convulsion, petrifaction and blazing eruption have, at bottom, the same origin: they are the outcome and expression of a faith in a God who is beyond the world and history.

This world comes alive and is immediately present in the story of Jesus, as told by the writers of the Gospels. All the characters who encounter Jesus bear the stamp of this world: the priest and the scribe, the Pharisee and the publican, the rich and the poor, the healthy and the sick, the righteous and the sinner. They appear in the story in a matter-of-fact and simple fashion, chosen at random and of great variety, and appearing in no particular order. Yet all the characters, however great their diversity, present a very human appearance. In their encounter with Jesus—whatever they experience in this encounter and whatever their attitude towards it—they come to this amazing event, their meeting with Jesus, as fully real people.

Jesus belongs to this world. Yet in the midst of it he is of unmistakable otherness. This is the secret of his influence and his rejection. Faith has given manifold expression to this secret. But even he who, prior to any interpretation, keeps his eyes fixed upon the historical appearance of Jesus, upon the manner of his words and works, even he meets with this his insoluble mystery. We become aware of the fact when we try to fit this figure into any of the descriptions and categories then prevalent in Judaism. He is a prophet of the coming kingdom of God. Indeed the title of prophet is occasionally used by the tradition (Mk. viii. 28; Mt. xxi. 11, 46, etc.). Yet he is in no way completely contained in this category, and differs from the customary ways of a prophet. A prophet has to produce his credentials, somewhat as did the prophets of the old covenant in telling the story of their calling and in accompanying their message with the sacred prophetic saying: ". . . says the Lord . . ." (Amos vi. 8, 14; Hos. ii. 16; xi. 11; Is. i. 24; and elsewhere). Jesus, on the other hand, never speaks of his calling, and nowhere does he use the ancient, prophetic formula. Even less do we find any trace of that self-justification typical of the apocalyptic visionaries of later Judaism, who claim the authority of ecstatic states of mind and visions, secret revelations of the next world, and miraculous insight into God's decrees. Jesus refuses to justify himself and his message in this way. But those who listen to him have to accept the saying: "And blessed is he who takes no offence at me" (Mt. xi. 6).

The prophet of the coming kingdom of God is at the same time a rabbi, who proclaims the divine law, who teaches in synagogues, who gathers disciples, and who debates with other scribes in the manner of their profession and under the same authority of scripture. The forms and laws of scribal tradition are to be found abundantly in his sayings. Prophet and rabbi—how does this go together? How does the message of the kingdom of God agree with the proclamation of the divine will? And what is the meaning of becoming a follower, and of the discipleship for which he calls, in view of this unity of prophet and rabbi? All these questions will concern us later.

This rabbi differs considerably from the other members of his class. Even external facts reveal this difference. Jesus does not only teach in the synagogues, but also in the open field, on the shores of the lake, during his wanderings. And his followers are a strange crowd. Even those people are amongst them whom an official rabbi would do his best to avoid: women and children, tax collectors and sinners. Above all, his manner of teaching differs profoundly from that of the other rabbis. A rabbi is an interpreter of Scripture. This lends authority to his office, an authority which has to prove itself from the given letter of Scripture and the not less authoritative exegesis of the "Fathers." Their authority is thus always a derived authority. Jesus' teaching, on the other hand, never consists merely in the interpretation of an authoritatively given sacred text, not even when words from Scripture are quoted. The reality of God and the authority of his will are always directly present, and are fulfilled in him. There is nothing in contemporary Judaism which corresponds to the immediacy with which he teaches. This is true to such a degree that he even dares to confront the literal text of the law with the immediately present will of God.[3]

We shall meet this feature again in his similes and parables, no less than in the words of wisdom which speak with manifest relevance and utmost simplicity: for example, that "a city set on an hill cannot be hid" (Mt. v. 14); that "men do not light a lamp and put it under a bushel" (Mt. v. 15); that "no one can add one cubit to his span of life" (Mt. vi. 27); that one should "let the day's own trouble be sufficient for the day" (Mt. vi. 34); etc. In all these utterances Jesus draws into the service of his message the world of nature and the life of man, and those everyday experiences which everyone knows and shares, without using the established structure of sacred traditions and texts. The listener is never obliged to look for premises which would give meaning to Jesus' teaching, or to recall the theory about doctrines and traditions which he would be supposed to know beforehand. For Jesus never talks *'over'* God, the world and man, the past and the future, from any particular "point of view."

This directness, if anything, is part of the picture of the historical Jesus. He bears the stamp of this directness right from the very beginning. The immediate present is the hallmark of all the words of Jesus, of his appearance and his actions, in a world which, as we said, had lost the present, because it lived between the past and the future, between traditions and promises or threats, in security or anxiety, conscious of its own rights or under sentence for its own lawlessness.

What the Gospels report on numerous individual occasions about Jesus' attitude to and influence on the different people he encounters is important in this context. We are not concerned here with the question whether all these scenes can claim historical reliability, how far we have to consider in them the influence of legends, and to what extent typical stylistic devices are used which are to be found elsewhere in the presentation of teaching and dis-

[3] Precisely these characteristics of Jesus' teaching, of course, raise the question as to whether the title of "rabbi" should be applied to him at all. So unlike is he to the "official rabbi." He may rather have impressed his hearers as a *popular teacher* who was also well acquainted with matters of the law [Ed.].

putes, of healings and the performance of various miracles. We have left no doubt that these factors do play a considerable part. Nevertheless, tradition has caught an essential feature of the historical Jesus, a feature which accords exactly with what we have said about his way of teaching.

Every one of the scenes described in the Gospels reveals Jesus' astounding sovereignty in dealing with situations according to the kind of people he encounters. This is apparent in the numerous teaching and conflict passages, in which he sees through his opponents, disarms their objections, answers their questions, or forces them to answer them for themselves. He can make his opponent open his mouth or he can put him to silence (Mt. xxii. 34). The same can be seen when he encounters those who seek help: miraculous powers proceed from him, the sick flock around him, their relatives and friends seek his help. Often he fulfils their request, but he can also refuse, or keep the petitioners waiting and put them to the test. Not infrequently he withdraws himself (Mk. i. 35ff.), but, on the other hand, he is often ready and on the spot sooner than the sufferers dare hope (Mt. viii. 5ff.; Lk. xix. 1ff.), and he freely breaks through the strict boundaries which traditions and prejudices had set up. Similar characteristics can be seen in his dealings with his disciples. He calls them with the command of the master (Mk. i. 16ff.), but he also warns and discourages them from their discipleship (Lk. ix. 57ff., xiv. 28ff.). Again and again his behaviour and method are in sharp contrast to what people expect of him and what, from their own point of view, they hope for. He withdraws from the people, as John reports, when he is to be made king (Jn. vi. 15). In his encounters with others we see time and again that he knows men and uncovers their thoughts, a feature which the Gospels have frequently elaborated to the point of the miraculous. The two sons of Zebedee meet with this quality when Jesus turns down their ambitious desires (Mk. x. 35ff.). Peter experiences it when, in answer to his confession of the Messiah, he is given Jesus' words about the suffering of the Son of Man, and when, wanting to make Jesus forsake his path, he receives the sharp retort: "Get behind me, Satan! For you are not on the side of God, but of men" (Mk. viii. 27-33).

2
Jesus' Preaching and Teaching

In the foregoing excerpts from Bornkamm's *Jesus of Nazareth* there is a heavy concentration on Jesus' *words.* If the Gospels do not offer us a consecutive chronological account of Jesus' career, can we be any surer that they give us the actual words spoken by Jesus? Here, too, the historian has to exercise caution—no doubt in adapting the reported sayings of Jesus to the developing practical needs of its daily life the Church modified many of them. Nevertheless not even the most radical critic would deny that the Gospels have preserved enough of the words actually uttered by Jesus to give us a reasonably clear picture of his preaching and teaching. That Jesus proclaimed the kingdom of God, that he spoke in parables, that he conveyed ethical instruction, that he was a teacher of wisdom, all of this is securely grounded in real history.

In this section no attempt will be made to present all of the words of Jesus that may fairly be judged authentic. Rather only typical examples from each of the different phases of his preaching and teaching will be given. The reader will find that sayings of Jesus are cited sometimes from Mark's Gospel, sometimes from Matthew or Luke. This is justified by the nature of the interrelationships of these three Gospels. One of the best-established tenets of modern Gospel criticism is the priority of Mark. Matthew and Luke were written later, and each in his own way used Mark as a basic source. But in addition to Mark, Matthew and Luke used also (as most scholars would agree) a collection of sayings of Jesus, which modern critics call Q, as we noted in the Introduction. Although Matthew and Luke were written considerably later than Mark, they have on occasion preserved a more nearly original form of a saying of Jesus than Mark because they were drawing on the sayings-source Q which is earlier in date than Mark's Gospel. This explains why in quoting words of Jesus we have recourse now to Mark, now to Matthew and/or Luke.

At the very heart of Jesus' message stands the announcement, "God's kingdom is near." The idea of the kingdom of God sounds strange and nebulous to our ears. But obviously Jesus felt free to introduce the news of the coming of God's kingdom to his hearers without any introduction or explanation. At the beginning of Mark's Gospel we read: "Now after John was arrested, Jesus came into Galilee, preaching the gospel of God and saying: 'The time is fulfilled, and the kingdom of God is at hand; repent, and believe in the gospel.' " (Mark 1:14-15)

The term "kingdom of God" was quite familiar to Jesus' first audience. It had a long history. The Psalmists had sung its praise:

> Thy kingdom is an everlasting kingdom, and thy dominion endures throughout all generations. (Psalm 145:13)
>
> The Lord has established his throne in the heavens; and his kingdom rules over all. (Psalm 103:19)

A number of other Psalms also are songs of celebration for the annual festival of the enthronement of the God of Israel as king over all the nations (e.g., Psalm 47, 93).

So in these more ancient hymns of praise Israel extolled God's dominion as a present reality. But in later Jewish thought, particularly in days of crisis and distress, the idea of the reign of God gathered up within itself also the hope of the Jewish people toward the future. Acknowledging in faith God's sovereign control over the world here and now, they at the same time waited with eager expectation for that day when God would finally and dramatically intervene in history to make his kingdom manifest to all men. They were living in tension, so to speak, between the "now" and the "then" of God's kingdom. Jesus' message of the kingdom of God, introduced by him so abruptly and without embellishment or elucidation, exhibits the same tension. On some occasions he speaks of the kingdom as if it were coming in the very near future, on others as if it were already present in and through his own ministry.

THE COMING OF THE KINGDOM OF GOD IN JESUS' PREACHING

The kingdom of God whose coming Jesus proclaims is not to be equated with the restoration of political fortunes so fondly expected by the Jewish people. Neither is it to be construed as the end product of a process of natural evolution. Nor again is it an ideal social goal to be realized by earnest moral endeavor on the part of men. Rather it is always and only God's coming gracious gift, dependent entirely on divine and not human power. The futurity of the kingdom is implicit in the prayer Jesus teaches his disciples:

> "Father, hallowed be thy name. *Thy kingdom come.* Give us each day our daily bread; and forgive us our sins, for we ourselves forgive everyone who is indebted to us; and lead us not into temptation." (Luke 11:2-4)

At the Last Supper, Jesus says to his disciples:

> "I have earnestly desired to eat this passover with you before I suffer; for I tell you I shall not eat it until it is fulfilled in the kingdom of God." And he took a cup and when he had given thanks he said, "Take this, and divide it among yourselves; for I tell you that from now on I shall not drink of the fruit of the vine until the kingdom of God comes." (Luke 22:15-18)

The Beatitudes also point to the impending victory of God:

> Blessed are you poor: for yours is the kingdom of God.
>
> Blessed are you that hunger now for you shall be satisfied.
>
> Blessed are you that weep now; for you shall laugh.
>
> (Luke 6:20f.)

In apocalyptic circles among the Jews of Jesus' day the future triumph of God was frequently depicted in cosmic imagery. Contemporary pictures of the dramatic events of the Last Days Jesus did not altogether reject. He too thought and spoke in terms of the fearful tribulations of the End time, the resurrection of the dead and the condemnation of the wicked, the coming of the Son of Man as judge of the world.

> "As it was in the days of Noah, so will it be in the days of the Son of Man. They ate, they drank, they married, they were given in marriage, until the day when Noah entered the

ark, and the flood came and destroyed them all. Likewise as it was in the days of Lot—they ate, they drank, they bought, they sold, they planted, they built, but on the day when Lot went out from Sodom fire and brimstone rained from heaven and destroyed them all—so will it be on the day when the Son of Man is revealed. On that day, let him who is on the housetop, with his goods in the house, not come down to take them away; and likewise let him who is in the field not turn back. Remember Lot's wife. Whoever seeks to gain his life will lose it, but whoever loses his life will preserve it. I tell you, in that night there will be two men in one bed; one will be taken and the other left. There will be two women grinding together; one will be taken and the other left." And they said to him, "Where, Lord?" He said to them, "Where the body is, there the eagles will be gathered together." (Luke 17:26-37)

"But take heed to yourselves lest your hearts be weighed down with dissipation and drunkenness and cares of this life, and that day come upon you suddenly like a snare; for it will come upon all who dwell upon the face of the whole earth. But watch at all times, praying that you may have strength to escape all these things that will take place, and to stand before the Son of Man." (Luke 22:34-36)

"For whoever is ashamed of me and of my words in this adulterous and sinful generation, of him will the Son of Man also be ashamed, when he comes in the glory of his Father with the holy angels." (Mark 8:38)

"But in those days, after that tribulation, the sun will be darkened, and the moon will not give its light, and the stars will be falling from heaven, and the powers in the heavens will be shaken. And then they will see the Son of Man coming in clouds with great power and glory. And then he will send out the angels, and gather his elect from the four winds, from the ends of the earth to the ends of the heaven." (Mark 13:24-27)

"When the Son of Man comes in his glory and all the angels with him, then he will sit on his glorious throne. Before him will be gathered all the nations, and he will separate them one from another as a shepherd separates the sheep from the goats, and he will place the sheep at his right hand, but the goats at the left." (Matthew 25:31-33)

Sometimes Jesus speaks of the kingdom as a feast to which his hearers are invited, but they reject the invitation because they are engrossed with worldly concerns:

> "A man once gave a great banquet, and invited many; and at the time for the banquet he sent his servant to say to those who had been invited, 'Come; for all is now ready.' But they all alike began to make excuses. The first said to him, 'I have bought a field, and I must go out and see it; I pray you, have me excused.' And another said, 'I have bought five yoke of oxen, and I go to examine them; I pray you, have me excused.' And another said, 'I have married a wife, and therefore I cannot come.' So the servant came and reported this to his master. Then the householder in anger said to his servant, 'Go out quickly to the streets and lanes of the city, and bring in the poor and maimed and blind and lame.' And the servant said, 'Sir, what you commanded has been done, and still there is room.' And the master said to the servant, 'Go out to the highways and hedges, and compel people to come in, that my house may be filled. For I tell you, none of those men who were invited shall taste my banquet.'" (Luke 14:16-24)

Apparently then Jesus did make use of the language and, to some extent, of the ideas of the apocalyptic visionaries of his age. But it should be noted that quite unlike them he emphatically refused to draw out elaborate portraits of the punishments of hell or the glories of heaven, or to calculate exactly the timetable of the Last Things. For him the kingdom of God was beyond human calculation, and could come only when God himself willed it. Men could do no more than make ready against the future that God would bring. The words and descriptions of Jesus have nothing in view but this one certainty, the "one pearl of great price"—God will reign.

> "Watch therefore, for you do not know on what day your Lord is coming. But know this, that if the householder had known in what part of the night the thief was coming, he would have watched and would not have let his house be broken into. Therefore you also must be ready; for the Son of Man is coming at an hour you do not expect." (Matthew 24:42-44)

> Being asked by the Pharisees when the kingdom of God was coming, he answered them, "The kingdom of God is not coming with signs to be observed; nor will they say, 'Lo, here it is!' or 'There!' for behold, the kingdom of God is in the midst of you." And he said to the disciples, "The days are coming when you will desire to see one of the days of the Son of Man, and you will not see it. And they will say to you, 'Lo, there!' or 'Lo, here!' Do not go, do not follow them. For as the lightning flashes and lights up the sky from one side to the other, so will the Son of Man be in his day." (Luke 17:20-24)

> "But of that day or that hour no one knows, not even the angels in heaven, nor the Son, but only the Father. Take heed, watch; for you do not know when the time will come. It is like a man going on a journey, when he leaves home and puts his servants in charge, each with his work, and commands the door-keeper to be on the watch. Watch therefore—for you do not know when the master of the house will come, in the evening, or at midnight, or at cockcrow, or in the morning—lest he come suddenly and find you asleep. And what I say to you I say to all: 'Watch.' " (Mark 13:32-37)

THE DAWNING OR THE PRESENCE OF THE KINGDOM OF GOD IN JESUS' PREACHING

In the sayings quoted above the kingdom of God is in the future. But the Gospels also contain many sayings of Jesus in which he summons his hearers to perceive that the kingdom is breaking in then and now in the very moment of his ministry. "The blind receive their sight and the lame walk, lepers are cleansed and the deaf hear, the dead are raised up and the poor have good news preached to them." (Matthew 11:5) All who have eyes to see must recognize that the event of God's reign is already taking place in Jesus.

> "Blessed are the eyes which see what you see! For I tell you that many prophets and kings desired to see what you see, and did not see it; and to hear what you hear, and did not hear it." (Luke 10:23-24)

The power of the demons is already being challenged by Jesus and Satan himself is falling to his doom.

> The seventy returned with joy, saying, "Lord, even the demons are subject to us in your name!" And he said to them, "I saw Satan fall like lightning from heaven. Behold I have given you authority to tread upon serpents and scorpions, and over all the power of the enemy; and nothing shall hurt you." (Luke 10:17-19)

Jesus, here as elsewhere, fuses the apocalyptic symbols of demons (believed by his contemporaries to be responsible for causing sickness and disease) and Satan and serpents and scorpions (representing the powers of evil) simply to bring home this one thing—the kingdom of God is actually irrupting into history in his words and deeds.

> "If it is by the finger of God that I cast out demons, then the kingdom of God has come upon you. When a strong man, fully armed, guards his own palace, his goods are in peace; but when one stronger than he assails him and overcomes him, he takes away his armor in which he trusted, and divides his spoil." (Luke 11:20-22)

Not only does Jesus summon his audience to realize how crucial is the present, he also connects their attitude toward him here and now with their status on the coming day of judgment of the Son of Man.

> "And I tell you, everyone who acknowledges me before men, the Son of Man also will acknowledge before the angels of God; but he who denies me before men will be denied before the angels of God." (Luke 12:8-9)

The presence of the kingdom of God in the words and deeds of Jesus was not of course an open fact that every casual bystander could plainly see. Only those "who had eyes to see and ears to hear" could catch it. Some in fact accused him of being possessed by the devil: "And when his friends heard it, they went out to seize him, for they said, 'He is beside himself.' And the scribes who came down from Jerusalem said, 'He is possessed by Beelzebub, and by the prince of the demons he casts out the demons.' " (Mark 3:21-22). Here it is made clear that the actualization of the reign of God in Jesus' ministry is certainly not a matter that anyone and everyone can grasp. Rather is the kingdom of God *hidden* in him. "Not in the way the apocalypticists thought, beyond the heavens, in the bosom of a mysterious future, but here, hidden in the everyday world of the present time, where no one is aware of what is already taking place. Of this Jesus speaks in his parables of the kingdom of God." (G. Bornkamm, *Jesus of Nazareth,* p. 69).

No historian today would seriously dispute that Jesus indeed extensively employed the method of teaching in parables. To be sure, in the process of transmission from their setting in the life of Jesus to their setting in the life of the early Church, the parables initially spoken by Jesus were gradually reshaped and expanded by the addition of allegorizing details. Evidently the Church wanted to extract the last ounce out of each parable by trying to find in every word and letter deep new spiritual meanings. But the parables as originally uttered by Jesus were not allegories. In an allegory the story itself is unimportant and does not ring true. So in one of Aesop's characteristic fables, when the fox cannot reach the grapes he wants and convinces himself they are sour grapes, we are dealing not with a real fox at all, since foxes do not eat grapes, but with hidden allusions to man's situation. Jesus' parables on the contrary always do ring true. They depict real life situations and the hearer does not have to probe beneath the surface for a variety of concealed meanings.

The Jewish rabbis of Jesus' time also taught in parables. But with them the parable was intended to illustrate a lesson or truth that was already contained in a written text or could be grasped independently of the story told in the parable. Jesus' parables, on the other hand, do not point to an ideal or truth that exists outside of themselves. They are in fact the direct and indispensable communicators of the truth Jesus means to affirm. In his parables Jesus addresses his hearers in the commonplace language of the everyday life of nature and man, of fields and fishing, sheep and goats, coins and lamps, workmen and bosses, savings and debts. And this ordinary language itself becomes the vehicle conveying his message of the nearness of God and putting men on the spot where they have to decide for or against.

So in the parables of "growth," of the mustard seed and the leaven, Jesus conveys to his hearers the mystery of the kingdom of God. These parables ought not to be read in terms of the modern concept of evolution. They do not indicate a process of development by which, under man's control, the kingdom of God is steadily extended. Rather do they confront men with the insignificant, obscure, and unrecognized beginnings of the kingdom of God in the words and acts of Jesus—beginnings all the same which contain within themselves the hope and promise of the coming glory of the kingdom to be bestowed by God alone.

> "The kingdom of God is as if a man should scatter seed upon the ground, and should sleep and rise night and day, and the seed should sprout and grow, he knows not how. The earth produces of itself, first the blade, then the ear, then the full grain in the ear. But when the grain is ripe, at once he puts in the sickle, because the harvest has come." (Mark 4:26-29).

Here the words "he knows not how" and "the earth produces *of itself*" underscore the fact that the kingdom is God's wonderful gift, not man's production. It is the same in the parables of the mustard seed and the leaven—out of next to nothing God marvelously consummates his purpose.

> Another parable he put before them, saying, "The kingdom of heaven is like a grain of mustard seed which a man took and sowed in his field; it is the smallest of all seeds, but when it has grown it is the greatest of shrubs and becomes a tree, so that the birds of the air come and make nests in its branches." He told them another parable. "The kingdom of heaven is like leaven which a woman took and hid in three measures of meal, till it was all leavened." (Matthew 13:31-33)

So the kingdom of God is already present in its mystery and hiddenness in the words and acts of Jesus, hiddenness inasmuch as the multitudes are unable to discern it.

> He also said to the multitudes, "When you see a cloud rising in the west, you say at once, 'A shower is coming'; and so it happens. And when you see the south wind blowing, you say, 'There will be scorching heat'; and it happens. You hypocrites! You know how to interpret the appearance of earth and sky; but why do you not know how to interpret the present time?" (Luke 12:54-56)

We have so far observed how the proclamation of the kingdom of God stands at the very center of Jesus' message. Now he confronts his hearers with its future coming, now with its apparently insignificant presence. The fact that Jesus seems to have thought of the kingdom *both* as future event *and* present reality has caused modern scholars quite a headache. Most troublesome has been the future element in his preaching. Since Jesus prophesied the impending arrival of the kingdom in the near future, and since, as history clearly shows, this did not happen, could he have been mistaken? More often than not the difficulty has been resolved by conveniently ignoring the futuristic evidence or by explaining it away as merely figurative language connoting continuing fellowship with God, or symbolizing eternal realities and an order beyond space and time.

On this whole question, three things need to be stressed. First, although Jesus seems to predict the coming of the kingdom of God in the very near future, he expressly repudiates all calculation of exact times and seasons and dates. "But of that day and hour no one knows, not even the angels of heaven, nor the Son, but the Father only." (Matthew 24:36). Second, to omit or to explain away the future element in Jesus' proclamation, because the actual non-arrival of the kingdom is embarrassing to modern theology, is to betray sound historical method. Third, in accordance with what is recorded in the Gospels, we simply must acknowledge the "both-and" in Jesus' message of the kingdom of God, *both* future *and* present. One of the best recent accounts of the interconnection of future and present in Jesus' pronouncements of the kingdom is that of Günther Bornkamm in *Jesus of Nazareth.*

GÜNTHER BORNKAMM: "FUTURE AND PRESENT" [1]

There is a remarkable tension, it would seem, between such sayings of Jesus as speak of the kingdom of God as a future happening, and such as announce its arrival now, in the present. "Thy kingdom come" is the second petition in the Lord's Prayer (Mt. vi. 10). "I shall not drink again of the fruit of the vine until that day when I drink it new in the kingdom of God," says Jesus to the disciples at the Last Supper (Mk. xiv. 25; Mt. xxvi. 29). A whole chain of such sayings is found in another place: "For as the light-

[1] G. Bornkamm, *op. cit.,* pp. 90-95. Reprinted by permission of the publisher.

ning flashes and lights up the sky from one side to the other so will the Son of man be in his day. . . . On that day, let him who is on the housetop, with his goods in the house, not come down to take them away; likewise let him who is in the field not turn back. Remember Lot's wife. . . . I tell you, in that night there will be two men in one bed; one will be taken and the other left. There will be two women grinding together; one will be taken and the other left. And they said to him, 'Where, Lord?' He said to them, 'Where the body is, there the eagles will be gathered together' " (Lk. xvii. 24-37). God's kingdom is future. That is why it is a question of "entering into the kingdom of God," into "life," into "joy." Sayings of this kind pervade all the Gospels. What is their relationship to the others, which announce the dawn, indeed the presence of God's kingdom today and now: "But if it is by the finger of God that I cast out demons, then the kingdom of God has come upon you" (Lk. xi. 20); "I saw Satan fall like lightning from heaven" (Lk. x. 18)? What is their relationship to the blessing of the eye-witnesses (Lk. x. 23f.), to the proclamation of the time of rejoicing (Mt. xi. 5f.; Mk. ii. 18ff., etc.)?

The attempts of the commentators to deal with this question are numerous. They have sought the aid of psychological explanations, and thought they observed various "moods" in Jesus himself. His prevailing mood, according to some, was one of expectation of the coming of the kingdom; but in the elation of enthusiasm and joy he could, in bold anticipation of the fulfilment, consider the present as the dawn of the kingdom. "There no longer exists for him any gulf between present and future; present and future, the ideal and reality are wedded together" (Bousset).[2] According to the others, this apparent contradiction is explained by the psyche of the prophet, who sees the future at one moment as present with us, and at another as stretching far ahead into distant time. But such attempts at explanation bring to the texts a point of view against which the texts themselves, without exception, rebel. They tear asunder what ought to hang together. For quite obviously the problem lies not in the fact that these pronouncements appear side by side, but that they are, paradoxical though it seem to us, closely interwoven.

[2] The reference is to W. Bousset, an earlier scholar of the History of Religions School, whose works *Kyrios Christos* and *Jesus* have remained quite influential [Ed.].

Not much better are biographical explanations which try to divide contradictory pronouncements into different periods in the thought and teaching of Jesus. Some would place those concerning the approach and presence of the kingdom in the latter part of his work; or, conversely, they would put them at the beginning and try to explain the actual sayings about the future on the basis of disappointment in this expectation, and the indefinite postponement of the final consummation. But this attempt, too, leads only to fantastic combinations and constructions which are not borne out by the texts.

Others, again, turn to differences in the transmission of Jesus' sayings, and acknowledge Jesus as the author of the sayings which deal with the presence of the kingdom of God and its development from a small beginning to magnificent completion, and say it was only the later Church, obviously reviving Jewish apocalyptic pictures and representations, which distorted the original message of Jesus. It is clear that this theory, too, can be reversed. Actually we ourselves observe again and again that we do have to reckon with such a process. Indeed it can be shown in the so-called synoptic apocalypse in Mark xiii that Jesus' own message is overlaid in no small degree by the later apocalyptic tradition of the Church. And yet, against this attempt, it must be said that in any case these criteria for making a distinction do not fit the facts. Just as we do not ascribe to Jesus merely the preaching of a "realised eschatology" (C. H. Dodd),[3] we should not make him an apocalypticist who merely renews the old expectations of late Jewish hopes in a more vivid form, and ascribe in either case the other view to the Church. Nor will it do to distinguish in the sayings of Jesus between real pronouncements and those of only "symbolic" importance, and understand the sayings about the future merely as metaphors for the "timeless" and "eternal."

None of these attempts at a solution leads to the goal. The reason for this failure might well lie in the wrong kind of question. We have seen already what decisive importance for the understanding of the kingdom of God in Jesus' preaching lies in these words: "The kingdom of God is not coming with signs to be observed" (Lk. xvii. 20). Therefore he who asks questions like these: What is

[3] C. H. Dodd was for long the most influential exponent of the view that according to the message of Jesus the kingdom of God was already present, already realized in history in his words and deeds [Ed.].

"happening" now and what will "happen" later? How much is taking place now? What will develop from these beginnings? What is the consummation like?—he who asks such questions has from the very start yielded to the temptation of making the kingdom of God something like a world phenomenon which can be observed and reckoned up. To be sure, no one can deny that Jesus' eschatological sayings, as far as they speak in the language and imagery of his time, about a definite happening now and in the future, are open to such an interpretation. And indeed there are people who set themselves to arrange the individual sayings of Jesus into conceptions comparable to our this-worldly mathematical calculations, and to make a sequence of this-worldly facts out of this, regardless of the usually grotesque result, and apparently justified by the large number of references which they can produce for every sentence. Yet nothing is gained here by a mere biblicism, and the elementary misunderstanding of Jesus' message is only too clear.

We must not separate the statements about future and present, as is already apparent from the fact that in Jesus' preaching they are related in the closest fashion. The present dawn of the kingdom of God is always spoken of so as to show that the present reveals the future as salvation and judgment, and therefore does not anticipate it. Again, the future is always spoken of as unlocking and lighting up the present, and therefore revealing today as the day of decision. It is therefore more than a superficial difference, more than one of degree, concerned, so to speak, only with the quantity of colour employed by the apocalyptic painter, when one notes that Jesus' eschatological sayings do not describe the future as a state of heavenly bliss nor indulge in broad descriptions of the terrors of the judgment. Hence in Jesus' preaching, speaking of the present means speaking of the future, and vice versa.

The future of God is *salvation* to the man who apprehends the present as God's present, and as the hour of salvation. The future of God is *judgment* for the man who does not accept the "now" of God but clings to his own present, his own past and also to his own dreams of the future. We might say with Schiller: "What we have denied the moment, eternity will never give back." Only here it applies in a new and fulfilled sense. In this acceptance of the present as the present of God, as we have tried to make clear, pardon and conversion are one in the works of Jesus.

God's future is God's call to the present, and the present is the time of decision in the light of God's future. This is the direction of Jesus' message. Over and over again, therefore, we hear the exhortation: "Take heed, watch" (Mk. xiii. 33-37; cf. 5, 9, 23, etc.). This "take heed to yourselves" (Mk. xiii. 9) stands in marked contrast to all curious questioning. Therefore, those very words of Jesus which refer to the future are not meant to be understood as apocalyptic instruction, but rather as eschatological promise, as W. G. Kümmel has pertinently observed.[4]

Certainly, in what has come down to us in the Gospels, there is no lack of sayings of an apocalyptic nature. They are gathered together in the thirteenth chapter of Mark's Gospel, taken up by Matthew and Luke and, especially by the latter, considerably remodelled. This so-called "synoptic apocalypse" is, however, a very complex composition. Undoubtedly traditional matter which has its origin in late Jewish apocalypticism has been taken over during the transmission of the synoptic material and set down as sayings of Jesus (sayings about war and rebellions, earthquakes and famines, darkness and falling stars, the laying waste of Judea and the desecration of the temple). Other sayings tell clearly of experiences of a later time (persecutions, false doctrines, seduction and so on). Unquestionably, too, genuine sayings of Jesus are interwoven with both. All this clearly has the intention of putting some chronological order into the sequence of the final events, and of making clear the "signs of the time" which give the hearer and reader a glimpse of the course of the world and its end. The whole chapter is therefore permeated with indications of time: "The end is not yet . . . this is but the beginning of sorrows . . . in those days . . . then . . . then . . ." This is not the place to determine which words of this apocalypse are to be ascribed to Jesus himself, a topic concerning which there is considerable disagreement on specific points. But it is clear that the speech as a whole is an apocalyptic composition, which even betrays itself as a literary production by the sentence "let the reader understand" (Mk. xiii. 14). Above all, we see from Luke, who in Chapter xxi. 20 (as also occasionally elsewhere) has read into the existing text the events of the Jewish war in the sixties in some detail, that the more and more detailed interpretation of just such speeches during their transmission was especially common. It is therefore difficult

[4] See W. G. Kümmel, *Promise and Fulfillment,* trans. Dorothea M. Barton (London, 1957) [Ed.].

to refrain from giving a critical judgment on the obvious tendency to set up as it were a "calendar" of the final events, in view of Jesus' own words which forbid such apocalyptic speculation. The quite varying history of the identification of the individual motifs of this "apocalypse" with ever new historical figures and events shows how questionable these assertions are. This is already seen by the time of the writing of the Gospels, but especially throughout the history of the Church up to our own times. In this way, for example, the apocalyptic utterance about the "desolating sacrilege" (Mk. xiii. 14, from Dan. ix. 27; xii. 11)—a mysterious symbol for the Antichrist who will penetrate into God's sanctuary and desecrate the temple—is applied in turn to Antiochus IV Epiphanes, through Caligula, Domitian and many names of the Middle Ages, on down to Napoleon and Hitler. Hence, the enlightened assertion that such explanations are typical manifestations, products of an excited apocalyptic fancy obsessed with the idea of the end of the world, seems to be very near the mark. One cannot dispute the relative validity of such a view, when one considers all the fanatical attempts to give, as it were, historical names to the stages which must be gone through as the world moves towards its end. But it is all too clear that even that enlightened standpoint proves itself, in the light of the message of Jesus, somewhat audacious. It attempts to look out at history as a whole from the higher watchtower of the observer; here, of course, in the opposite sense to apocalypticism, in that it denies any relation whatsoever of history and the present to God's future.

Thus we are brought back again to the "Take heed, watch!", which noticeably pervades even this "apocalypse" of the Gospels. Jesus' message demands that we reckon with the future, lay hold on the hour, do not calculate the times. Those who wait in the right way are therefore called to fulfil the will of God now with all their might.

THE ETHICAL TEACHING OF JESUS

Jesus appeared, as we have seen, with a message of the coming kingdom of God, and so the title of "prophet" could be applied to him (see Mark 8:28; Matthew 21:11, 46; Luke 7:16, 39, etc.). But he came upon the scene also like a rabbi. He is occasionally addressed as "rabbi." (Mark 9:5; 10:51; 11:21; 14:45), and like other rabbis he teaches in the synagogue, has a circle of pupils around him, and discusses with opponents or enquirers matters pertaining to the Law. To the question, "Which is the chief commandment?" (Mark 12:28-34), for instance, Jesus answered in good rabbinic fashion, as the famous Rabbi Hillel had also answered—love to God and to one's neighbor.[5]

Now if Jesus expected and proclaimed the coming of God's kingdom any minute, why should he have bothered to assume the role of a "learned Doctor," concerned to give instruction on the Law and ethical obedience? The Gospels offer no explanation of how these two phases of his activity were connected in the mind of Jesus himself. Consequently there has been much scholarly speculation. A usual solution has been to portray Jesus as one possessed of an intuitive awareness of God's will and so as first and foremost an ethical teacher summoning men to radical obedience—in which case his proclamation of the coming kingdom of God could be regarded as adventitious and secondary. But it is just as likely that Jesus first and foremost believed and preached that God's reign was near and summoned his hearers to penitence, faithfulness, and preparedness in the face of it. We now know that the combination of apocalyptic fervour with strenuous dedication to the Law was not without precedent in Jesus' day—the community of Qumrân understood themselves *both* to be engaged in the warfare of the Last Days *and* to be devotees of the Law in its entirety.

Certainly Jesus comes before us in the Gospels as both herald of the kingdom of God and ethical teacher in the rabbinic mold.

A whole series of sayings of Jesus, some of which are now set down here, have parallels among the rabbis and reveal his continuity with rabbinic Judaism.

> "Therefore I tell you, do not be anxious about your life, what you shall eat or what you shall drink, nor about your body, what you shall put on. Is not life more than food, and the body more than clothing? Look at the birds of the air: they neither sow nor reap nor gather into barns, and yet your heavenly Father feeds them. Are you not of more value than they?" (Matthew 6:25-26)

> "Judge not that you be not judged. For with the judgment

[5] Whether the title "rabbi" really fits Jesus is open to debate (see above pp. 42-43).

you pronounce you will be judged, and the measure you give will be the measure you get." (Matthew 7:1-2)

"Are not two sparrows sold for a penny? And not one of them will fall to the ground without your Father's will. But even the hairs of your head are all numbered. Fear not, therefore; you are of more value than many sparrows." (Matthew 10:29-30)

"Will any one of you, who has a servant plowing or keeping sheep, say to him when he has come in from the field, 'Come at once and sit down at table'? Will he not rather say to him, 'Prepare supper for me, and gird yourself and serve me, till I eat and drink; and afterward you shall eat and drink'? Does he thank the servant because he did what was commanded? So you also, when you have done all that is commanded you, say, 'We are unworthy servants; we have only done what was our duty.' " (Luke 17: 7-10)

"What then of the man who hears these words of mine and acts upon them? He is like a man who built his house upon the rock; and the rain fell, and the floods came, and the winds blew and beat upon that house, but it did not fall, because it had been founded on the rock. And everyone who hears these words of mine and does not do them will be like a foolish man who built his house upon the sand; and the rain fell, and the floods came, and the winds blew and beat against that house, and it fell; and great was the fall of it." (Matthew 7:24-27)

At other points also Jesus shows his continuity with rabbinic Judaism, by appealing to the injunctions of the Law as set forth in the Old Testament Scripture.

And as he was setting out on his journey, a man ran up and knelt before him and asked him, "Good Teacher, what must I do to inherit eternal life?" And Jesus said to him, "Why do you call me good? No one is good but God alone. You know the commandments: 'Do not kill, Do not commit adultery, Do not steal, Do not bear false witness, Do not defraud, Honor your father and mother.' " (Mark 10:17-19)

And one of the scribes came up and heard them disputing with one another, and seeing that he answered them well,

> asked him, "Which commandment is the first of all?" Jesus answered, "The first is, 'Hear, O Israel. The Lord our God, the Lord is one; and you shall love the Lord your God with all your heart, and with all your soul, and with all your mind, and with all your strength.' The second is this, 'You shall love your neighbor as yourself.' There is no other commandment greater than these." (Mark 12:28-31)

And if Matthew 5:17 can be taken as an authentic saying of Jesus and not as a reflection of the later Christian community's questions about the Law's validity, then here Jesus expressly affirms his own positive attitude toward the Law.

> "Think not that I have come to abolish the law and the prophets; I have come not to abolish them but to fulfil them." (Matthew 5:17)

For all this, the designation "rabbi" is quite unable to embrace all of Jesus' activity as ethical teacher. He was a much more informal figure than the traditional rabbis. Unlike them he numbered women among his followers and had a special affection for children. He was unconventional enough to consort with the riff-raff, and to sit down at table with tax collectors, sinners, and prostitutes (Luke 7:39).

But above all Jesus adopts at times toward the Law of Moses an authoritatively critical attitude that no rabbi would have ventured. This is evident in the antitheses of the Sermon on the Mount ("But I say unto you"), where he asks for an obedience to the will of God that goes beyond the prescribed demands of the Law.

> "You have heard that it was said to the men of old, 'You shall not kill; and whoever kills shall be liable to judgment.' But I say to you that everyone who is angry with his brother shall be liable to judgment." (Matthew 5:21-22)

> "You have heard that it was said, 'An eye for an eye and a tooth for a tooth.' But I say to you, Do not resist one who is evil. But if anyone strikes you on the right cheek, turn to him the other also; and if anyone would sue you and take your coat, let him have your cloak as well; and if anyone forces you to go one mile, go with him two miles." (Matthew 5:38-41)

> "You have heard that it was said, 'You shall love your neighbor and hate your enemy.' But I say to you, Love your enemies and pray for those who persecute you." (Matthew 5:43-44)

Here, as Bornkamm puts it, Jesus "liberates the will of God from its petrifaction in tables of stone, and reaches for the heart of man which seeks seclusion and safety behind the stronghold of observance of the law." (*Jesus of Nazareth,* p. 105). The concreteness and simplicity of Jesus' commands, in which "God is always present and so is man," strike a fateful blow at the pedantry and casuistry of Jewish legalism, which at its worst hedges life about with an intricate web of restrictions and prohibitions. Nowhere is this more obvious than in the contempt Jesus shows for contemporary Jewish disputations about the minutiae of Sabbath observance.

> One sabbath he was going through the grainfields; and as they made their way his disciples began to pluck ears of grain. And the Pharisees said to him, "Look, why are they doing what is not lawful on the sabbath?" And he said to them, "Have you never read what David did, when he was in need and was hungry, he and those who were with him: how he entered the house of God, when Abiathar was high priest, and ate the bread of the Presence, which it is not lawful for any but the priests to eat, and also gave it to those who were with them?" And he said to them, "The sabbath was made for man, not man for the sabbath." (Mark 2:23-27)

So on such subjects as the sabbath, ritual cleanliness (Mark 7:14-23), and divorce (Mark 10:2-9), Jesus claims a remarkable freedom quite unprecedented among the rabbis over against the Jewish Law. It should not surprise us that he incurred the odium and antagonism of the Pharisees and the scribes. Though the Gospels come from a time when the hostility between the synagogue and the Christian congregations had become greatly intensified, there is no reason to doubt their substantial historical trustworthiness when they depict Jesus himself in open conflict with the Pharisees and the scribes.

The latter frequently tried to trap Jesus with loaded questions, none more loaded than the famous question about tribute money.

> And they sent to him some of the Pharisees and some of the Herodians, to entrap him in his talk. And they came and said to him, "Teacher, we know that you are true, and care for no man; for you do not regard the position of men, but truly teach the way of God. Is it lawful to pay taxes to Caesar or not? Should we pay them, or should we not? But knowing their hypocrisy, he said to them, "Why put me to the test? Bring me a coin, and let me look at it." And they brought one. And he said to them, "Whose likeness and inscription is this?" They said to him, "Caesar's." Jesus said to them, "Render to Caesar the things that are Caesar's, and to God the things that are God's." (Mark 12:13-17)

"Render to Caesar the things that are Caesar's, and to God the things that are God's." The history of interpretation of this saying is marked by a bewildering variety of opinions—that Jesus here counsels an attitude of permissiveness and acceptance toward the ruling political power and so defends the sovereign rights of the state; that he draws a rigid line of division between religion and politics; that he sets the higher "law of God" above the laws of the state and so tacitly endorses political subversion. But from the slender clues afforded here (or for that matter in the rest of the New Testament) it would be absurd to build up any particular political philosophy. This is all the more so since in the form that Jesus' answer takes the "rendering to Caesar" is consigned to the margin, so to speak, and all the weight of emphasis falls on the "rendering to God the things that are God's."

The background of the saying is of course the unrest of the Jews under political subjection to Rome and under the burden of taxation, here in particular the poll tax payable from subject provinces to the imperial treasury. Nevertheless the main thrust and intention of Jesus' reply is nonpolitical or suprapolitical—the Roman denarius which is handed to Jesus bears the image of Caesar and rightly belongs to him, and so in paying it back to Caesar men are *as a matter of course* simply giving him his own: but since men bear the image of God, they ought *as a matter of choice or decision* to surrender themselves to the will of God. Caesar exists as a fact of everyday life. But his rule, like all ephemeral political forces, passes away: God's reign comes and remains and knows no end; and with its abiding reality Jesus challenges his hearers to link their lives.

Just as here Jesus takes a commonplace object of daily life, a Roman coin, and makes it witness for his audience to God's rule and God's claim upon them, so also in many other sayings he allows the created world just as it is to speak eloquently to his hearers of the Creator God and his will.

> "He makes his sun to rise on the evil and on the good, and sends rain on the just and on the unjust." (Matthew 5:45)

> "Therefore I tell you, do not be anxious about your life, what you shall eat or what you shall drink, nor about your body, what you shall put on. Is not life more than food, and the body more than clothing? Look at the birds of the air; they neither sow nor reap nor gather into barns, and yet your heavenly Father feeds them. Are you not of more value than they? And which of you by being anxious can add one cubit to his span of life? And why are you anxious about clothing? Consider the lilies of the field, how they grow; they neither toil nor spin; yet I tell you, even Solomon in all his glory was not arrayed like one of these. But if God so clothes the grass of the field, which today is and tomorrow is thrown into the oven, will he not much more clothe you, O men of little faith?" (Matthew 6:25-30)

> "If you then, who are evil, know how to give good gifts to your children, how much more will your father who is in heaven give good things to those who ask him!" (Matthew 7:11)

As the last two quotations make plain (Matthew 6:25-30 and Matthew 7:11), Jesus allows the common everyday world to point not merely to God the Creator, but to God *the Father*. The naming of God as Father was not of course new with Jesus. Long ago Israel, believing that God had elected her as his special people, had thought of herself as the first-born son of God (Exodus 4:22-33), and elsewhere God is called the Father of Israel (Jeremiah 30:9). But Jesus brought the Fatherhood of God to the very center of his message, and presented it not as a truth inherent in the past history of the Jewish people but as an event of God's grace that could only be responded to and appropriated in and through his (Jesus') words here and now. This is what the parable of the prodigal son is all about.

> "The younger son gathered all he had and took his journey into a far country, and there he squandered his property in loose living. . . . But when he came to himself he said '. . . I will arise and go to my father, and I will say to him, "Father, I have sinned against heaven and before you; I am no longer worthy to be called your son; treat me as one of your hired servants." ' And he arose and came to his father. But while he was yet at a distance, his father saw him and had compassion, and ran and embraced him and kissed him. . . . The father said to his servants, 'Bring quickly the best robe, and put it on him; and put a ring on his hand, and shoes on his feet; and bring the fatted calf and kill it, and let us eat and make merry; for this my son was dead, and is alive again; he was lost, and is found.' "

So far in the story the father dominates the center of the stage. He freely divides the inheritance between his sons. Even in the squalid life to which the younger son sinks in the far country, he is haunted still by memory of his father's love—"I will arise and go to my father." On his return it is the father who takes the initiative and runs to greet him and calls for a joyous celebration.

Only from this point on is the stage given to the elder brother, who now learns from one of the servants the reason for the feasting and music and dancing.

> "But he was angry and refused to go in. His father came out and entreated him, but he answered his father, 'Lo, these many years I have served you, and I never disobeyed your command; yet you never gave me a kid that I might make merry with my friends. But when this son of yours came, who has devoured your living with harlots, you killed for him the fatted calf!' And he said to him, 'Son, you are always with me, and all that is mine is yours. It was fitting to make merry and be glad, for this your brother was dead, and is alive; he was lost, and is found.' " [see Luke 15:11-32 for the whole parable]

The elder brother's tragedy is precisely that he is unable to see the event of God's fatherly and forgiving love toward the wayward and errant that is taking place before his very eyes, and so in his own self-righteousness is excluded from the joy of acknowledging that the reign of the Father God is already dawning. As Jesus communicates it, therefore, the Fatherhood of God is not an abstract proposition or a timeless general truth, but an event that occurs in and with his very words and deeds for those who have "ears to hear and eyes to see."

The nearness of God as an event taking place manifests itself also in the prayer language of Jesus. In prayer Jesus addresses God as Abba. Abba is an Aramaic intensive form of the word for "Father," and connotes an intimacy and familiarity of relationship. Such usage of Abba was scarcely reverential enough for the rabbis of Jesus' day. The ministry of the historical Jesus is so obviously complex and difficult to grasp as a whole that it would be unwise to set too much store by a single word. Yet better than any other word this one word Abba—Father—seems to sum up Jesus' own sense of his vocation and mission—to bring God's fatherly love close to those whom he encounters.

> "And he said, 'Abba, Father, all things are possible to thee; remove this cup from me; yet not what I will, but what thou wilt.' " (Mark 14:36)

Here for Jesus himself the word Abba could not come easily—it is connected with the grim destiny he is persuaded is in store for him. No more for the believer is the Fatherhood of God ever an easy natural fact that can at any time be comprehended by all. Not out of their own resources, but only through the power of the "Spirit" in their hearts can the believers cry, "Abba, Father!" (Romans 8:15; Galatians 4:6).

Everywhere in his message Jesus allows his words to authenticate themselves. His words carry the indelible stamp of their own authority. Very seldom, in order to support his words by some imprimatur from outside, does he enlist the help of past traditions or past institutions or regulative texts out of the old Scripture. In his use of the word "Amen" in numerous sayings, he reveals the sovereign freedom with which he speaks. The word "Amen" originally stood as the response of the Jewish congregation to a prayer uttered in their presence. Jesus transfers it from the end to the beginning of his sayings, as if to confirm by solemn asseveration the urgency and the validity of what he is about to say—"Amen (verily) I say unto you." There are thirty examples of this singular usage in Matthew's Gospel alone, e.g.

> "For truly [Amen], I say to you, till heaven and earth pass away, not an iota, not a dot will pass from the law until all is accomplished." (Matthew 6:2)

> "Thus, when you give alms, sound no trumpet before you as the hypocrites do in the synagogues and in the streets, that they may be praised by men. Truly [Amen] I say to you, they have their reward." (Matthew 6:2)

In the light of this "Amen" alone, coming at the beginning of Jesus' prophecies and commands so abruptly to Jewish ears, it is no wonder that he impressed his contemporaries as speaking with an authority far greater than that of the Pharisees and scribes.

Finally, let us note that nowhere does Jesus' authority and freedom of speech stand out more clearly than in the parable of the Good Samaritan. On being asked by a certain lawyer, "Who is my neighbor?", Jesus answered with this story.

> "A man was going down from Jerusalem to Jericho, and he fell among robbers, who stripped him and beat him, and departed, leaving him half dead. . . . A priest . . . and a Levite passed by on the other side. But a Samaritan . . . came to where he was: and when he saw him, he had compassion . . . and brought him to an inn and took care of him . . . which of these three, do you think, proved neighbor to the man who fell among the robbers?" He said, "The one who showed mercy on him." And Jesus said to him, "Go and do likewise." (Luke 10:29-37)

The story is told in the most matter of fact way, and reads like a notice in the evening paper. There is no romanticizing. Nothing is said about the motives of the priest or Levite in passing by the wounded man. Nor is the Samaritan praised at all for his virtue. Jesus tells quite simply how only the Samaritan stops and goes out of his way to minister to the need of the poor fellow left lying by the roadside. Now of course the Samaritan who does all this happens to be the member of a despised race of people. And the parable ends not with the Samaritan's congratulating himself on his kindly act, but with a question—"Which of these three, do you think, proved neighbor to the man who fell among the robbers?" The lawyer had begun with his own question, "Who is my neighbor?"

At the close Jesus has turned everything right around, "Yes that was your question. But do not ask patronizingly about the ones to whom it is your duty to show benevolence. Instead put yourself in the position of the unfortunate man in the ditch waiting for a true 'neighbor' to bring you help. Only then will you learn that the whole business of the 'neighbor' has to do with uncalculated and spontaneous deeds of kindness and of charity."

Without warning or apology and with characteristic directness Jesus introduces the despised Samaritan into this whole question of the "neighbor." Confronted with the plain goodness of the hated one, the lawyer is forced to examine himself and his calculating and legalistic brand of religiosity. Though we are not told about the lawyer's final response, there is little doubt that by such a parable Jesus could only have scandalized legalistic Jewish listeners.

One recalls reading of an American lecturer describing how the priest and the Levite passed by on the other side, and it was left to a member of the despised Samaritan race to carry through the simple duty of kindness to the wounded man. Then he concluded, "Murmur among the crowd: We'll get this guy Jesus one day."

And they did in the end.

3

Jesus' Journey to Jerusalem—The Way to Death

The Gospels all set the activity of Jesus in two different localities, in Galilee in the northland of Palestine and in the city of Jerusalem.

In Galilee Jesus called disciples to follow him (e.g. Mark 1:16-20). While there are indications in the Gospel tradition that the early Church read some of its own experiences back into the situation of the historical Jesus' disciple group, there is little question that he did have his band of followers, and that he wanted them to share not only his task and his travail but also his authority—"I will make you become fishers of men" (Mark 1:17: the disciples are commissioned to "hook" men for the coming kingdom of God). Some of Jesus' hardest sayings are on the theme of discipleship, e.g. "Do not think that I have come to bring peace on earth; I have not come to bring peace but a sword." (Matthew 10:34); "No one who puts his hand to the plough and looks back is fit for the kingdom of God." (Luke 9:62).

Mark was responsible for locating in Galilee numerous nature miracles and wonderful works of healing on the part of Jesus described as exorcisms (it should be remembered that in Jesus' day and place disease was attributed to the activity of demons). It seems very likely that the nature miracles represent legendary embellishment of the tradition by the early Church. While the historian perhaps ought not to make any a priori *judgment about the possibility or impossibility of miracles, it is very important to observe that Jesus himself consistently refused to perform miracles as signs of his authority—"Truly, I say to you, no sign shall be given to this generation." (Mark 8:12). Quite probably, however, Jesus did in fact effect cures among the sick in mind and body. These cures he saw not as the accomplishments of a skilled psychiatric healer but as challenges to faith, faith in the redemptive action of God breaking in through his words and deeds. Conceivably the miraculous element in Mark's Gospel goes back to the misty memories of peasant folk in Galilee, among whom Jesus had left the impression of being a wonder-worker.*

In Galilee the road was not altogether smooth for Jesus. The movement he initiated there had its ups and downs. The Gospels tell of popular support but also of opposition not only among the crowd but also in high places, from the ruler, Herod Antipas. Quite early Mark records a decision of Jesus' enemies to put him to death (Mark 3:6). All in all there is no ground for describing Jesus' Galilean ministry (as some of the earlier Lives did) as a beautiful springtime idyll.

What then of Jesus' move from Galilee to Jerusalem? The Gospel of John suggests several journeys of Jesus between Galilee and Jerusalem; the Synoptic Gospels suggest that Jesus' one visit to Jerusalem was his last visit and compress the events of his ministry there into a very short space of time. There is no easy solution as to which is the more accurate version. What is not in doubt is that Jesus' decision to go to Jerusalem was the great crisis of his life, and that the early Church recognized its significance and reflected deeply on it.

M. GOGUEL: WHY THE DEPARTURE FROM GALILEE TO JERUSALEM? [1]

The Gospels do not give a clear or coherent record of the circumstances under which Jesus left Galilee to go to Jerusalem. There is the hint that he finally set out from Galilee in order to avoid the pursuit of Herod—some Pharisees are reported to have come to him with the warning: "Get away from here, for Herod wants to kill you." (Luke 13:31). But for the most part the memory of his movement to Jerusalem and of the reasons for it was soon obscured by the idea, prevalent in the early Church, that Jesus went up to Jerusalem with the specific purpose of accomplishing his death in accordance with the divine plan.

M. Goguel gives a concise account of the three stages through

[1] Maurice Goguel, *Jesus and the Origins of Christianity. Vol. II: The Life of Jesus,* trans. Olive Wyon (New York: Harper & Row, Publishers, 1960), p. 399. Reprinted by permission of George Allen & Unwin Ltd.

which the tradition of his departure from Jerusalem has developed.

A comparison of the various data which we have tried to discover by the analysis of the Gospel narratives relating to the departure of Jesus from Galilee enables us to discover the development of tradition on this point. Originally, people thought that Jesus had left Galilee owing to the hostility of Herod, and because the precautions which he had taken in order to be able to carry on his work proved insufficient. Soon, however, the Early Church could not be satisfied with this manner of presenting events; the Christians felt that something as important as going up to Jerusalem could not have been imposed upon Jesus by external constraint, and they felt uneasy at the suggestion that he had yielded to the threats of Herod. So they came to the conclusion that Jesus went up to Jerusalem either in order to continue his work of preaching in a more important sphere (this is John's account), or, in order to give himself up to a Messianic manifestation, to make a triumphal entry into the city, and to be welcomed there as the One who "cometh in the Name of the Lord." At the third stage, finally, it seemed that, in going up to Jerusalem, Jesus could not have been ignorant of what was going to happen there. Thus he left Galilee knowing that he would meet the Cross in the Holy City, and in consequence that in going up to Judaea he would fulfil the divine purpose. The triumphal march was then transformed into a march to execution; at the same time, all the details in the story which represent him as hoping that his message would win the hearts of the people of Jerusalem, or even as fleeing from Herod, have not been entirely effaced from the record.

It is sometimes said that if the idea of going up to Jerusalem purposely to die had in fact been Jesus' own and not part of the early Church's theology, then he must simply be understood as a man of distinct suicidal tendency. That may be so. Yet quite possibly Jesus did ponder at length the harsh and bitter fate of many of the prophets before him and did reckon with the possibility that his own mission would involve him in a violent end. Quite possibly, therefore, the recurrent predictions Jesus makes of his coming suffering, rejection, and death in Mark's Gospel (e.g. Mark 8:31) are not entirely prophecies after the event created by the Church but do contain a historical kernel. Almost certainly Jesus went up to Jerusalem in order to bring home to the very heart of the ancestral citadel of Jewish faith his message of the coming kingdom of God: and almost certainly he was well aware of the dire peril attendant on the enterprise.

G. BORNKAMM: THE ENTRY INTO JERUSALEM AND THE CLEANSING OF THE TEMPLE [2]

The story of the Triumphal Entry, as it is called (the first Palm Sunday), is reported in all the Gospels (see Mark 11:1-11 and parallels). The Gospels give the impression that Jesus intended the entry as a Messianic demonstration. But since nowhere else in the tradition is Jesus depicted as making overt claims to Messiahship, it is more likely that some of the crowd of pilgrims gathered in Jerusalem for the Passover Festival interpreted or misinterpreted the arrival of Jesus and his group as a signal for the start of a Messianic uprising. This would accord with the hostility of the city authorities to him and his execution as a criminal.

The story of the Cleansing of the Temple is also recorded in all the Gospels, although placed by John very early in Jesus' public ministry (see Mark 11:15-18 and parallels). What is involved here is not merely Jesus' vexation over the secularization of the seat of Jewish worship and ritual, but an act of purification of the Temple in readiness for the coming reign of God.

G. Bornkamm's short assessment of these two episodes is helpful.

Jesus' entry into Jerusalem in the company of his followers forms part of this last chapter of his life (Mk. xi. 1ff.). It is the time of the Passover, when huge masses of pilgrims gather in the holy city to celebrate the liberation of the people from Egypt, and and eschatological hopes run high, as we also know from later testimonies.

[2] G. Bornkamm, *Jesus of Nazareth,* pp. 158-159. Reprinted by permission of the publisher.

The expectation of the coming kingdom of God also fills the heart of Jesus and his companions, who celebrate him, the prophet from Galilee, and acclaim him as the Messiah. It is controversial in how far Jesus himself intended this entry as a demonstration that he was the Messiah. Later tradition has, at any rate, understood the entry in this sense, and endowed it with miraculous features which bestow upon it this meaning. However, even if we here take into consideration the subsequent belief of the disciples, upon whom the deeper meaning of the events did not dawn until Jesus had been "glorified" (Jn. xii. 16), even then this entry of Jesus and his followers would be inconceivable without his powerful claim that the kingdom of God is dawning in his word, and that the final decision will turn upon himself. The struggle against the spiritual leaders of the nation was thereby opened by himself.

This is also borne out by the cleansing of the temple (Mk. xi. 15ff.), which follows upon the entry into Jerusalem. It, too, is soon "overexposed" to the beam of Messianic expectation, as can be seen from the rendering in John (ii. 13ff.). And yet, according to the synoptic Gospels, it is more than an act of reform intended simply to restore the temple service to its original purity. The scene that Jesus saw in the outer temple court was not particularly offensive to a Jew. It is in keeping with the activities which up to the present day attend all pilgrimages. Merchants and money-changers do their business, offer for sale beasts for sacrifice, and exchange the foreign money of the pilgrims into ancient Hebrew or Phoenician currency, which was prescribed for commerce and the temple dues. Care was taken, as we know, that the sacred parts of the temple were not touched by this. But Jesus, brandishing his scourge, puts an end to these activities, and cleanses the sanctuary for the approaching kingdom of God. Here, too, we must not disregard this real context of what happened, nor the claim upon which this action is founded. With good reason, then, all the Gospels connect the story of the cleansing of the temple with Jesus' dispute with the leaders of the nation about the "authority" which entitles him to this action (Mk. xi. 27ff.).

THE TRIAL OF JESUS

The story of the Passion proper opens with a chronological note at Mark 14:1, which has no connection with anything that goes before it: "It was now two days before the Passover and the feast of Unleavened Bread." It seems that the Passion narrative, because of its extreme importance for the faith and theology of the Church, was the first part of the Gospel story to be set down in writing as an ordered and coherent whole. The space given to it and the emphasis put upon it largely justify the opinion that the Gospels are "Passion reports with extended introductions."

Here, however, just where the historian would want to know exactly the actual course of events leading up to the death of Jesus, is his task most difficult, for most of all in the Gospels has the Passion story been influenced by the doctrine of the Church. The early Christians drew no distinction between the facts of the Passion story and their significance for faith, and in telling the story they were never tired of appealing to the Old Testament to prove that Jesus' death had been foretold there (e.g. Luke 22:37: "For I tell you that this scripture must be fulfilled in me, 'And he was reckoned with transgressors.'" See Isaiah 53:12).

In the Passion story the Trial narratives are preceded by the Last Supper of Jesus with his disciples (see Mark 14:17-25 and parallels). In this regard there is a significant discrepancy in chronology between John's Gospel and the Synoptics. John's Gospel points to the 14th of Nisan, according to the Jewish calendar, as the day of Jesus' death, the day the Passover lambs were slaughtered. In this case the Last Supper of the preceding evening is not a Passover meal. The Synoptics on the contrary regard the Last Supper as a Passover meal taken on the evening of Thursday 14th Nisan, in which case Jesus died on the cross on 15th Nisan. A voluminous literature exists on this chronological question, but it remains unsolved. The Gospel texts on the Last Supper all reflect the theology and liturgy of the early Church. Nevertheless we can deduce from them that Jesus himself most probably understood the meal as an anticipation of the Messianic banquet in the coming kingdom of God (see Mark 14:25).

After the Supper, events follow each other in rapid succession, the kiss of the betrayer and the arrest in Gethsemane, the trial before the Jewish High Court, the Sanhedrin, the appearance before Pilate, and the crucifixion.

The Trial reports of the various Gospels (see Mark 14:53ff. and parallels) reveal significant discrepancies, and opinions differ widely about their historicity. Some hold that they are complete fabrications, others that they contain a substantial nucleus of history. On the latter supposition the question arises, among others, about the relative responsibility of Jews and Romans for the condemnation and death of Jesus, a question lately given considerable publicity by the discussion in the Second Vatican Council leading up to the decision to absolve the Jews from the charge of "deicide."

In his recent book On the Trial of Jesus *(Berlin: Walter de Gruyter and Co., 1961), the Jewish scholar Paul Winter stresses the obvious fact that the Trial reports betray the early Church's tendency to exculpate Pilate and the Romans and blame the Jews, and develops the view that since the Sanhedrin in Jesus' time possessed competence to try capital cases and so had no need to have recourse to Pilate for the execution of Jesus, and since in fact Jesus was executed in the Roman fashion, as laid down by Roman law, the whole story of the hearing before the Jewish High Court is unhistorical. On the other hand the classical scholar, A. N. Sherwin-White* (Roman Society and Roman Law in the New Testament, *Oxford:Clarendon Press, 1963) defends the view that in Jesus' day the Sanhedrin had no jurisdiction in capital cases, that the Sanhedrin session and the condemnation for blasphemy are historical, and that the Jewish leaders then turned to Pilate and put pressure on him, if not on the political charge of sedition against Jesus then on the religious charge.*

A sort of compromise view is soberly presented in the following extract from M. Goguel's Life of Jesus. *The historicity of the Sanhedrin hearing as well as the Sanhedrin's non-competence in capital cases are upheld, but the initiative for the arrest of Jesus and so on is ascribed to Pilate and the Romans.*

M. GOGUEL: "JEWS AND ROMANS" [3]

Many factors have influenced the Gospel story; in the case of the Passion narrative, however, another element—which has little or no influence on the rest of the Gospel story—must be taken into account. When we compare the four records of the trial of Jesus we see that one idea which is definitely suggested in Mark is

[3] M. Goguel, *The Life of Jesus,* pp. 464-474. Reprinted by permission of George Allen & Unwin Ltd.

emphasized far more strongly in Matthew and in Luke, and above all in John. The idea is this: that although it is true that Pilate passed sentence on Jesus and actually carried it out, it was the Jews who were responsible for his death, that it was they who forced the Procurator to condemn him to death; indeed, that Pilate would have released him if his hand had not been forced by the Jewish authorities and by the angry mob which they had stirred up by their suggestions. Mark mentions Pilate's effort to give Jesus the benefit of the special pardon granted to some criminal at the time of the Passover (Mark xv. 6f.); he notes that Pilate knew that the Jews had delivered him up "for envy" (xv. 10). Luke emphasizes this point and makes Pilate declare to the high priest: "I find no fault in this man" (xxiii. 4), and in the episode of Barabbas he says quite plainly that Pilate wished to release Jesus (xxiii. 20). When the Jews refused to listen to this proposal, he makes Pilate reiterate his declaration of the innocence of Jesus: "Why, what evil hath he done? I have found no cause of death in him" (xxiii. 22). In the account in Matthew, Pilate's wife sends him an urgent warning even while he is actually on the judgment seat: "Have thou nothing to do with that just man: for I have suffered many things this day in a dream because of him" (xxvii. 19); and when the Procurator pronounces the sentence he washes his hands before the people, saying: "I am innocent of the blood of this just person: see ye to it." To which the crowd replies: "His blood be on us and on our children" (xxvii. 24-25). In John, Pilate formally declares twice over the innocence of Jesus (xviii. 38, xix. 6), and it is still more evident than in the Synoptic narrative that in condemning Jesus to death he is yielding to the pressure of the people, and to the fears that he might be accused at Rome for not being "Caesar's friend," because he had released an aspirant to the royal power (xix. 12).

As time went on this tendency increased. In the Gospel of Peter Pilate washes his hands, just as in the Gospel of Matthew, but it is added that neither Herod nor the Jews washed their hands, and that it was Herod who pronounced and carried out the sentence (1-2). The narrator emphasizes these details by saying that when Joseph of Arimathea went to ask for the body of Jesus, Pilate sent him on to Herod (3-4).

Later, still more weight was laid upon the testimony given by Pilate to the innocence of Jesus. Tertullian says that he was *jam pro sua conscientia christianus* (*Apol.*, XXI); Origen (*Contra Celsum,* II, 34) asserts that it was the Jewish authorities rather than Pilate who sentenced Jesus to death, and in the *De Principiis* (IV, 8) he uses this phrase: "The Jews nailed him to the cross." The Epistle of Barnabas, Melito of Sardis, Aristides, Irenaeus, and others use terms which, although they do not actually say that it was the Jews who condemned and crucified Jesus, at least suggest that they were entirely responsible for his death.

There are several reasons for the growth of this tendency to absolve the Romans and Pilate of the responsibility for the death of Jesus, and to throw the entire blame for it upon the Jews. First of all, it reflects the fact that the real cause of the Passion was the hostility of the Jewish authorities towards Jesus; it is also due, however, to the opposition which existed, from the very earliest days of the life of the Church, between Jews and Christians. Very naturally, the Christians would think that as the Jews were their sworn foes, they must also have been the enemies of their Master; on the other hand, they would naturally conceive the Roman attitude towards Jesus to have been the one to which they were accustomed: a somewhat contemptuous indifference. They would also see an analogy between the rejection of the Gospel by the Jews and the rejection of Jesus himself. From another point of view, the tendency to relieve the Romans of responsibility was due to a necessity of apologetics. The One whom the Christians presented to the world as the messenger of God and the Saviour had been sentenced to death by a Roman tribunal. This fact created difficulties for the preaching of the Gospel in the Roman world, for it might give the impression that to be converted to the Christian Faith meant taking the side of a rebel, and therefore to be in revolt against the Imperial authority. Hence the Christians were anxious to prove that the Procurator who had sent Jesus to execution had been convinced of his innocence, and that he had publicly announced that he had been forced to yield to the irresistible pressure of the populace and of the Jewish authorities. Christianity was not always in conflict with the Roman Empire. Before the moment when the conflict broke out of which the Johannine Apocalypse (Book of Revelation) remains the typical document (especially in its thirteenth chapter), a conflict which was to last until the time of Constantine, there was a period in which Christianity was definitely loyal to the Empire, and regarded the Roman power as a power established by God in order to maintain order in the world. (Cf. Rom. xiii. 1-7.)

The existence of a friendly attitude towards the Romans within primitive Christianity explains some of the modifications in detail to which the Passion narrative was subjected from Mark to John and even to pseudo-Peter. The question therefore must be faced: was this influence already present in the Marcan narrative? And can it be that all the other passages which mention the part played by the Jews and Romans respectively have been altered by this idea? Careful examination of this question is all the more necessary because the manner in which the Gospel narratives present the part played by the Sanhedrin and by Pilate in the trial of Jesus are not free from inconsistencies and obscurities, and do not seem to be in accord with the legal administration of Palestine under the government of Procurators.

The main theme of the Gospel record is this: Jesus is arrested on the initiative of the Jewish authorities. It is they who decide to take action against him (Mark xiv. 1-2), who receive with joy the proposal of Judas, which will make it easier for them to carry out their plans (Mark xiv. 10-11). It is they who send to Gethsemane a band of men armed with swords and staves (Mark xiv. 43). When Jesus is arrested, he is brought before the high priest. The Sanhedrin assembles, interrogates Jesus, and after it has extracted a declaration from him, the members of the Council declare unanimously that he is worthy of death (Mark xiv. 53, 55-64). In the mind of the narrator this amounts to a death sentence. Immediately after the sitting of the Sanhedrin Jesus is actually treated not as an accused person, but as a condemned criminal. This is manifested in the scene of the outrages which he suffers at the hands of the agents of the Sanhedrin and the servants of the high priest (Mark xiv. 65). The Synoptic Gospels do not say why the sentence which has just been pronounced is not carried out immediately. It does not seem doubtful that the reason why the Roman trial follows the Jewish trial is, according to them, that which is suggested by the Fourth Gospel, when the Jews say to Pilate (who advises them to try Jesus themselves): "It is not lawful for us to put any man to death" (John xviii. 31). It seems strange that the Jews need to remind the Procurator of the limits which the Roman power has placed to their rights; it is no less strange that the Synoptic Gospels do not explain clearly the necessity for the second trial, when we cannot suppose that they were writing for readers who were familiar with Palestine affairs. Thus the source followed by Mark may have presented the report of the two trials in a different way from that in which the evangelists understood it, or it may not have explained it at all. In any case, so far as the evangelists are concerned, their theory is pure conjecture.

When Jesus appears before Pilate, the Jewish authorities, the chief priests, and the elders of the people play the part of accusers, and, supported by the fanatical crowd, force the Procurator to pass the sentence of death (Mark xv. 1-15).

This arrangement of the Gospel records raises two questions. First of all, is it a unity? that is, can it contain all the elements of the story? Further, does it agree with what we know about the legal administration of Palestine in the time of the Procurators?

In John's account of the arrest of Jesus, both at the beginning and at the end, he mentions the presence of the cohort and of the centurion. "Judas, taking the cohort and the agents of the chief priest and the Pharisees . . ." (xviii. 3). "The cohort, the centurion and the agents of the Jews seized Jesus, bound him, and led him away" (xviii. 12). The philo-Roman tendency being still stronger in the Fourth Gospel than in the Synoptic Gospels, it is impossible to suppose that the cohort and the centurion have been introduced into the narrative by John. Thus we must admit that he is here following a source which mentioned a collaboration between the Jews and the Romans, or which may have mentioned the Romans only. The Jews will have been added by the evangelist under the influence of the Synoptic narratives.

We shall have to return to these hypotheses later. *A priori,* however, it seems very unlikely that the Jews and the Romans would have co-operated to arrest Jesus. Whether that be so or not, if the Romans did proceed to arrest Jesus, or if they merely collaborated, the initiative, or at least part of the initiative, must be assigned to them. In consequence, the Gospel narrative which attributes this initiative wholly to the Jews is a biased perversion of the primitive tradition.

If the trial before Pilate had taken place under the conditions described by the evangelists, it would have been of a very special character. Pilate would not have had to condemn or acquit Jesus, but merely either to ratify the sentence passed by the Sanhedrin or to forbid its being carried out. Now, in the whole account of the

Roman trial there is no allusion whatever to the Jewish trial, nor to its conclusion. In the two instances the accusation is not the same. Before the Sanhedrin Jesus is accused of blasphemy, which is a religious crime; before Pilate he is charged with wishing to make himself king of the Jews. It is of course true that the two accusations are not wholly unconnected. The second, however, might be understood as a transposition of the first into language intelligible to a Roman. But in the hypothesis before us there seems no necessity for such a transposition. If the course of events was such as is here described, Pilate would not have needed to enquire whether Jesus had committed acts which could be punished by Roman law; all he would have had to do would have been to find out whether he had really committed offences which were punishable under the Jewish law, and then see that they were correctly applied. In this case, however, there is no question of a Jewish sentence sanctioned by the Roman authority, but both the sentence and the execution were carried out by the Romans in accordance with Roman Law.

One of the leading ideas in the Gospel story of the Roman trial is the passionate clamour of the Jewish populace for the death of Jesus. In the Gospel of Luke, however, there is a trace of a tradition which contradicts this idea. When Jesus is being led away to be crucified, Luke says:

> And there followed him a great company of people, and of women, which also bewailed and lamented him. But Jesus turning unto them said, Daughters of Jerusalem, weep not for me, but weep for yourselves and for your children.

This is followed by a prophecy of the destruction of Jerusalem which ends thus:

> If they do these things in a green tree, what shall be done in the dry? (Luke xxiii. 27-32).

After Jesus has drawn his last breath, again Luke says:

> And all the people that came together to that sight, beholding the things which were done, smote their breasts and returned. (Luke xxiii. 48).

Thus a tradition existed according to which the death of Jesus was felt by the people as a disaster. Thus the general scheme of the narrative, which seems to have been that of the evangelists, is not developed in a logical manner; here and there in their record we can discern elements which imply differing traditions about the trial of Jesus.

Does the theory of the two trials harmonize with what we know of the legal administration in the time of the Procurators? Mommsen[4] says quite definitely "Yes." He believes that, in essentials, the Marcan narrative is accurate (*kaum betrübt*). In his opinion Jesus was sentenced by the Sanhedrin in regular order, but that he had to appear before Pilate because, although in accordance with the principles of their policy in dealing with conquered peoples they had allowed the Jewish legal system to remain in existence, the Romans, in order to avoid the Sanhedrin becoming the tool of an anti-Roman policy, had reserved to themselves a right of control by taking away from them the right to pass capital sentences without the approval of the Procurator.

In the work *Sanhedrin* (I, 18*a,* 37),[5] an anonymous *baraïta*[6] says that "forty years before the destruction of the Temple the right of pronouncing capital sentences was taken away from Israel." It does not seem necessary to take this piece of evidence quite literally. The right which had been taken away from the Sanhedrin was not the right of passing capital sentences but that of carrying them out without a preliminary approval by the Romans. Until the eve of the war, instances occurred in which Jewish sentences were pronounced and carried out. Rabbi Eliezer ben Zadok, who died before 130 of our era, tells that when he was a child he was present at the execution of the daughter of a priest, who was burned alive because she had been convicted of adultery (*Sanh.,* 7, 2, 52*b*). Josephus (*G. J.* II, xi. 6, ¶ 220)[7] says that until Cuspius Fadus and Tiberius Alexander, that is to say, until the year 48, the Procurators

[4] Theodor Mommsen (1811-1903) was one of the most famous modern historians of classical antiquity. His *Roman History,* published in 1854-56, revealed his very extensive knowledge of epigraphy and Roman Law and superseded previous works [Ed.].

[5] *Sanhedrin* is one of the tractates of the Mishnah, the great collection of oral traditions relating to the Law passed on among the Jewish rabbis and assembled at the beginning of the third century A.D. See the English translation of the Mishnah by H. Danby, Oxford, 1933 [Ed.].

[6] *Baraïta* is an Aramaic word denoting a tradition of the Tannaim (*i.e.,* the rabbinic teachers of the oral law in the period A.D. 70-220) *not* incorporated in the Mishnah. The evidence about Sanhedrin jurisdiction in the baraïta cited by M. Goguel has been much disputed [Ed.].

[7] The reference is to Josephus' *The Jewish War.*

did not disturb the Jewish customs. After that date the Roman administrators did not alter the legal system itself, but from time to time they would interfere, and irritate the feelings of their subjects.

Regnault[8] has opposed the theory of Mommsen by dwelling on the difficulties which would have been introduced by the system of having two trials in direct succession, in cases where the Jewish law and the Roman law did not impose the same penalty, or did not agree on the nature of a crime or a misdemeanour. From this he concludes that when the administration of the Procurators was established the jurisdiction of the Sanhedrin must have been forbidden in the sphere of criminal law.

This objection would carry weight only if the control of the Procurator could be conceived solely in the form of a Roman trial, independent of the Jewish trial, and following it. But this system would have led to the actual suppression of national Jewish institutions, and this would have been contrary to the policy of the Roman Empire. The Procurator simply had to assure himself that the rules of the Jewish Law were being correctly applied, and to see that the Sanhedrin did not use the power which had been left in its hands as a weapon against the Roman administration.

To the argument from theory Regnault adds an argument from fact. Josephus (*A.J.*, XX, 9, 1, ¶¶ 200-203)[9] reports that in 62, between the death of Festus and the arrival of his successor Albinus, the high priest Ananias assembled the Sanhedrin and brought before it James the brother of Jesus and some other individuals, who were condemned to death and executed. Certain Jews went to meet Albinus and accused the high priest of having acted illegally, and the Procurator admitted that their complaint was well founded. Regnault concludes from this that the Sanhedrin could not be assembled without the consent of the Procurator, and that therefore it was no longer an independent tribunal. But, as Juster, in particular, has proved,[10] the narrative of Josephus contains certain inaccuracies. Between the death of Festus and the arrival of his successor there cannot have been a real lapse of the Roman authority in Jerusalem. If it had really been illegal to call the Sanhedrin together, Albinus (knowing what we do of his character) would most

[8] The reference is to Regnault, *Une province procuratorienne au début de l'Empire romain: Le procès de Jésus-Christ* (Paris, 1909), pp. 64ff.

[9] The reference is to Josephus' *Antiquities of the Jews* [Ed.].

[10] Juster, *Les Juifs dans l'Empire romain,* II, 141ff.

certainly have exercised his prerogative and have imposed certain penalties. Probably all that he said was that it would have been more fitting to await his arrival instead of hurrying the matter through with the approval of the sentence of the Sanhedrin by the acting governor.

No one would dispute the fact that until the destruction of Jerusalem the Sanhedrin remained the competent authority in all matters of secondary importance. It cannot always have been easy to see in advance whether a case was going to be sufficiently serious for the Sanhedrin to know whether the penalty it would inflict would be within its powers or not. There is only one possible and logical solution, and it is this: that the Sanhedrin had preserved intact the right to judge a case, but that the capital sentences which it might pronounce could not be carried out before they had received the approval of the governor.

The approval necessary for the carrying out of the sentence imposed by the Sanhedrin did not mean that a Roman trial had to follow a Jewish trial, or that a Roman penalty was added to the Jewish penalty; the case of James and that of the priest's daughter, reported in the work entitled *Sanhedrin,* prove this. Thus Mommsen's theory about the legal system in Palestine in the time of the Procurators seems to be well founded. The condemnation of Jesus by the Sanhedrin, followed by the approval of the Procurator, seems to have been theoretically possible. There are, however, two reasons which prevent us from thinking that this was the actual course of the trial of Jesus. The first is this: the Roman trial, as it is described in the Gospels, is not represented as the control of the Jewish trial but as a second trial, quite independent of the first one, on an entirely different charge. The second is that the penalty inflicted is Roman and not Jewish.

Although the Sanhedrin was competent to try Jews who did not possess the rights of Roman citizenship, its jurisdiction did not annul or limit the *jus gladii,* which was one of the prerogatives of the Procurators. The governor retained the right to prosecute, to try, and to execute whom he would. The trial of Jesus could have been conducted solely under the orders of the Procurator, on his own initiative, without any intervention on the part of the Sanhedrin at all, or with a merely semi-official consultation with this tribunal or with some of its members.

In light of these considerations, Goguel envisages the course of events as having developed in the following way (see The Life of Jesus, *pp. 480-482). From the first moment of the proceedings against Jesus the Romans as well as the Jews were involved. The Gospels have preserved no recollection of any conferences between the Procurator and the Jews, presumably because of the tendency in the tradition to whitewash Pilate and because such conferences must have been held in secret. But the fact that such conferences did take place may be inferred from Mark 15:2, where Pilate proceeds immediately to question Jesus when he is led before him without the Jewish authorities having brought up any charge against him.*

That Jesus appeared before the Sanhedrin and was adjudged guilty of blasphemy and worthy of death we may take to be historical. But it was Pilate who, provoked by the Jews, ordered the arrest of Jesus as a political agitator. *Most probably the Procurator insisted that if at the prompting of the Jewish religious authorities he had Jesus condemned to death, they would not cause a disturbance among the people or inform Rome that he had shed the blood of an innocent man. From the Sanhedrin Pilate required an explicit assurance to that effect.*

THE DEATH OF JESUS

The accounts of the death of Jesus in the Gospels are all heavily overlaid with the faith and theology of the primitive Church. We need refer only to Mark's report that at the very moment of Jesus' death "the curtain of the temple was torn in two from top to bottom" (Mark 15:38). This is hardly a historical reminiscence, but rather a symbolic representation of the significance of Jesus' death for Christian believers as a means of access to the innermost sanctuary of God's presence.

M. Goguel gives an excellent summary statement of what actually happened.

It is not surprising that very early the narrative of the death of Jesus received all kinds of developments and additions. The sections which have been added are easy to recognize, and when they are eliminated the primitive tradition which remains is very simple. It told how Jesus was taken to Golgotha and crucified, after (according to the usual custom) he had been offered some drugged wine. A *titulus* was placed upon the cross which made known that he had been condemned as King of the Jews, then the soldiers divided his garments among themselves. After a time of agony which was comparatively short, since it lasted only three hours, Jesus, having lamented that God had deserted him, yielded up his spirit.[11]

In all the Gospels the story of Jesus' death is followed by short accounts of the burial and then by the Easter texts, witnessing to the empty tomb and the resurrection. The Easter texts belong more to the life and faith of the early Church than to the history of Jesus. In the Easter stories, the compilers of the Gospel tradition are not so much concerned to relate what actually happened with the accuracy of a police report as to proclaim Christ's victory over death and sin and to document the believers' faith in his victorious power. To say so much is not necessarily to deny that shortly after the death of Jesus something decisive happened to convince his followers of his continuing presence.

But with the witness to the empty tomb and the resurrection appearances we are in an order of reality that will not allow empirical verification. In short, with the Easter texts we have passed over from the history of the man Jesus of Nazareth to the history of the believing Church.

[11] M. Goguel, *The Life of Jesus,* p. 545. Reprinted by permission of George Allen & Unwin Ltd.

PART TWO

NINETEENTH CENTURY LIBERAL VIEWS OF JESUS

4

Ernest Renan's Life of Jesus

In Part One we put the last stage first—on the basis of the most recent and most advanced phase of Gospel criticism we drew out a sketch of the minimal historical features of Jesus' ministry. Such a sketch may provide a sort of control point from which to evaluate earlier and more expansive views of Jesus.

We took note in the Introduction of the cultural and historical factors that paved the way for the Leben-Jesu-Forschung *or the Life of Jesus movement of the nineteenth century. Intellectual revolt against the tyranny of dogma had a good deal to do with the rise of research into the life of the man Jesus. It is hard for us now to imagine the pathos attaching to the labors of those who in one way or another participated in the revolt.*

Despite the existence of earlier German "Lives" the first to take the results of German criticism and apply them to a full-scale biography of Jesus as entirely human was the distinguished French orientalist, Ernest Renan. Born at Tréguier in Brittany in 1823, he was brought up as a Catholic and initially intended for the priesthood. He took another way. In 1862 he became professor of Hebrew and Semitic Languages at the Collège de France. A year later his Vie de Jésus *was published. Catholic sentiments were so outraged that he was suspended from his professorial duties by the Government, and when the French ministry offered him a post in the Bibliothèque Impériale, he turned it down with scorn.*

The Vie de Jésus *was written in a limpid French prose style and, aside from everything else, had a fascinating literary appeal. The book proved very popular. Sixty thousand copies were sold in the first six months. Renan offered his readers, as Schweitzer remarks, "a Jesus who was alive, whom he, with his artistic imagination, had met under the blue heaven of Galilee, and whose lineaments his inspired pencil had seized."*

JESUS, VILLAGE *ILLUMINÉ* [1]

Jesus was born at Nazareth, a small town of Galilee, which before his time had no celebrity. All his life he was designated by the name of "the Nazarene," and it is only by a rather embarrassed and round-about way, that, in the legends respecting him, he is made to be born at Bethlehem. We shall see later the motive for this supposition, and how it was the necessary consequence of the Messianic character attributed to Jesus. The precise date of his birth is unknown. It took place under the reign of Augustus, about the Roman year 750, probably some years before the year 1 of that era which all civilized people date from the day on which he was born.

The name of *Jesus,* which was given him, is an alteration from *Joshua.* It was a very common name; but afterward mysteries, and an allusion to his character of Saviour, were naturally sought for in it. Perhaps he, like all mystics, exalted himself in this respect. It is thus that more than one great vocation in history has been caused by a name given to a child without premeditation. Ardent natures never bring themselves to see aught of chance in what concerns them. God has regulated everything for them, and they see a sign of the supreme will in the most insignificant circumstances.

The population of Galilee was very mixed as the very name of the country indicated. This province counted amongst its inhabitants, in the time of Jesus, many who were not Jews (Phœnicians, Syrians, Arabs, and even Greeks). The conversions to Judaism were not rare in these mixed countries. It is therefore impossible to raise here any question of race, and to seek to ascertain what blood flowed in the veins of him who has contributed most to efface the distinction of blood in humanity.

[1] E. Renan, *The Life of Jesus* (New York: The Modern Library, Inc., 1927), pp. 81-83, 97-98. All selections reprinted by permission of the publisher.

He proceeded from the ranks of the people. His father, Joseph, and his mother, Mary, were people in humble circumstances, artisans living by their labor, in the state so common in the East, which is neither ease nor poverty. . . .

His distinctive character very early revealed itself. Legend delights to show him even from his infancy in revolt against paternal authority, and departing from the common way to fulfill his vocation. It is certain, at least, that he cared little for the relations of kinship. His family do not seem to have loved him, and at times he seems to have been hard toward them. Jesus, like all men exclusively preoccupied by an idea, came to think little of the ties of blood. The bond of thought is the only one that natures of this kind recognize. "Behold my mother and my brethren," said he, in extending his hand toward his disciples; "he who does the will of my Father, he is my brother and my sister." The simple people did not understand the matter thus, and one day a woman passing near him cried out, "Blessed is the womb that bare thee, and the paps which gave thee suck!" But he said, "Yea, rather blessed are they that hear the word of God, and keep it." Soon, in his bold revolt against nature, he went still further, and we shall see him trampling under foot everything that is human, blood, love, and country, and only keeping soul and heart for the idea which presented itself to him as the absolute form of goodness and truth.

THE GALILEAN IDYLL [2]

With consummate literary skill Renan paints his highly lyrical and romantic portrait of the Galilean ministry of Jesus. One may think of the portrait as extremely subjective, a travesty of what the Gospel texts are actually saying, and yet be deeply moved by its aesthetic power.

Such was the group which, on the borders of the lake of Tiberias, gathered around Jesus. The aristocracy was represented there by a customs officer and by the wife of one of Herod's stewards. The rest were fishermen and common people. Their ignorance was extreme; their intelligence was feeble; they believed in apparitions and spirits. Not one element of Greek culture had penetrated

[2] E. Renan, *op. cit.,* pp. 184-193.

this first assembly of the saints. They had very little Jewish instruction; but heart and goodwill overflowed. The beautiful climate of Galilee made the life of these honest fishermen a perpetual delight. They truly preluded the kingdom of God—simple, good, and happy—rocked gently on their delightful little sea, or at night sleeping on its shores. We do not realize to ourselves the intoxication of a life which thus glides away in the face of heaven—the sweet yet strong love which this perpetual contact with nature gives, and the dreams of these nights passed in the brightness of the stars, under an azure dome of infinite expanse. It was during such a night that Jacob, with his head resting upon a stone, saw in the stars the promise of an innumerable posterity, and the mysterious ladder by which the angels of God came and went from heaven to earth. At the time of Jesus the heavens were not closed, nor the earth grown cold. The cloud still opened above the Son of man; the angels ascended and descended upon his head; the visions of the kingdom of God were everywhere, for man carried them in his heart. The clear and mild eyes of these simple souls contemplated the universe in its ideal source. The world unveiled perhaps its secret to the divinely enlightened conscience of these happy children, whose purity of heart deserved one day to behold God.

Jesus lived with his disciples almost always in the open air. Sometimes he got into a boat, and instructed his hearers, who were crowded upon the shore. Sometimes he sat upon the mountains which bordered the lake, where the air is so pure and the horizon so luminous. The faithful band led thus a joyous and wandering life, gathering the inspirations of the master in their first bloom. An innocent doubt was sometimes raised, a question slightly sceptical; but Jesus, with a smile or a look, silenced the objection. At each step—in the passing cloud, the germinating seed, the ripening corn—they saw the sign of the kingdom drawing nigh, they believed themselves on the eve of seeing God, of being masters of the world; tears were turned into joy; it was the advent upon earth of universal consolation.

"Blessed," said the master, "are the poor in spirit: for theirs is the kingdom of heaven.

"Blessed are they that mourn: for they shall be comforted.

"Blessed are the meek: for they shall inherit the earth.

"Blessed are they which do hunger and thirst after righteousness: for they shall be filled.

"Blessed are the merciful: for they shall obtain mercy.

"Blessed are the pure in heart: for they shall see God.

"Blessed are the peacemakers: for they shall be called the children of God.

"Blessed are they which are persecuted for righteousness' sake: for theirs is the kingdom of heaven."

His preaching was gentle and pleasing, breathing Nature and the perfume of the fields. He loved the flowers, and took from them his most charming lessons. The birds of heaven, the sea, the mountains, and the games of children, furnished in turn the subject of his instructions. His style had nothing of the Grecian in it, but approached much more to that of the Hebrew parabolists, and especially of sentences from the Jewish doctors, his contemporaries, such as we read them in the *"Pirkê Aboth."* His teachings were not very extended, and formed a species of sorites in the style of the Koran, which, joined together, afterward composed those long discourses which were written by Matthew. No transition united these diverse pieces; generally, however, the same inspiration penetrated them and made them one. It was, above all, in parable that the master excelled. Nothing in Judaism had given him the model of this delightful style. He created it. It is true that we find in the Buddhist books parables of exactly the same tone and the same character as the Gospel parables; but it is difficult to admit that a Buddhist influence has been exercised in these. The spirit of gentleness and the depth of feeling which equally animate infant Christianity and Buddhism, suffice perhaps to explain these analogies.

A total indifference to exterior life and the vain appanage of the "comfortable," which our drearier countries make necessary to us, was the consequence of the sweet and simple life lived in Galilee. Cold climates, by compelling man to a perpetual contest with external nature, cause too much value to be attached to researches after comfort and luxury. On the other hand, the countries which awaken few desires are the countries of idealism and of poesy. The accessories of life are there insignificant compared with the pleasure of living. The embellishment of the house is superfluous, for it is frequented as little as possible. The strong and regular food of less generous climates would be considered heavy and disagreeable. And as to the luxury of garments, what can rival that which God has given to the earth and the birds of heaven? Labor in climates of this kind appears useless; what it gives is not equal to what it costs. The animals of the field are better clothed than the most opulent man, and they do nothing. This contempt, which, when it is not caused by idleness, contributes greatly to the elevation of the soul, inspired Jesus with some charming apologues: "Lay not up for yourselves treasures upon earth," said he, "where moth and rust doth corrupt, and where thieves break through and steal, but lay up for yourselves treasures in heaven, where neither moth nor rust doth corrupt, and where thieves do not break through nor steal: for where your treasure is, there will your heart be also. No man can serve two masters: for either he will hate the one and love the other; or else he will hold to one and despise the other. Ye cannot serve God and Mammon. Therefore I say unto you, take no thought for your life, what ye shall eat, or what ye shall drink; nor yet for your body, what ye shall put on. Is not the life more than meat, and the body than raiment? Behold the fowls of the air: for they sow not, neither do they reap, nor gather into barns; yet your heavenly Father feedeth them. Are ye not much better than they? Which of you by taking thought can add one cubit unto his stature? And why take ye thought for raiment? Consider the lilies of the field, how they grow; they toil not, neither do they spin; and yet I say unto you, That even Solomon in all his glory was not arrayed like one of these. Wherefore, if God so clothe the grass of the field, which to-day is, and to-morrow is cast into the oven, shall he not much more clothe you, O ye of little faith? Therefore take no thought, saying, What shall we eat? or, What shall we drink? or, Wherewithal shall we be clothed? For after all these things do the Gentiles seek; for your heavenly Father knoweth that ye have need of all these things. But seek ye first the kingdom of God, and his righteousness; and all these things shall be added unto you. Take therefore no thought for the morrow: for the morrow shall take thought of the things of itself. Sufficient unto the day is the evil thereof."

This essentially Galilean sentiment had a decisive influence on the destiny of the infant sect. The happy flock, relying on the heavenly Father for the satisfaction of its wants, had for its first principle the regarding of the cares of life as an evil which choked the germ of all good in man. Each day they asked of God the bread for the morrow. Why lay up treasure? The kingdom of God is at hand. "Sell that ye have and give alms," said the master. "Provide yourselves bags which wax not old, a treasure in the heavens that faileth not." What more foolish than to heap up treasures for heirs whom thou wilt never behold? As an example of human folly, Jesus loved to cite the case of a man who, after having enlarged his barns and amassed wealth for long years, died before having enjoyed it! The brigandage which was deeply rooted in Galilee, gave much force to these views. The poor, who did not suffer from it, would regard themselves as the favored of God; whilst the rich, having a less sure possession, were the truly disinherited. In our societies, established upon a very rigorous idea of property, the position of the poor is horrible; they have literally no place under the sun. There are no flowers, no grass, no shade, except for him who possesses the earth. In the East, these are gifts of God which belong to no one. The proprietor has but a slender privilege; nature is the patrimony of all.

The infant Christianity, moreover, in this only followed the footsteps of the Essenes, or Therapeutæ, and of the Jewish sects founded on the monastic life. A communistic element entered into all these sects, which were equally disliked by Pharisees and Sadducees. The Messianic doctrine, which was entirely political among the orthodox Jews, was entirely social amongst them. By means of a gentle, regulated, contemplative existence, leaving its share to the liberty of the individual, these little churches thought to inaugurate the heavenly kingdom upon earth. Utopias of a blessed life, founded on the brotherhood of men and the worship of the true God, occupied elevated souls, and produced from all sides bold and sincere, but short-lived attempts to realize these doctrines.

Jesus, whose relations with the Essenes are difficult to determine (resemblances in history not always implying relations), was on this point certainly their brother. The community of goods was for some time the rule in the new society. Covetousness was the cardinal sin. Now it must be remarked that the sin of covetousness, against which Christian morality has been so severe, was then the simple attachment to property. The first condition of becoming a disciple of Jesus was to sell one's property and to give the price of it to the poor. Those who recoiled from this extremity were not admitted into the community. Jesus often repeated that he who has found the kingdom of God ought to buy it at the price of all his goods, and that in so doing he makes an advantageous bargain. "The kingdom of heaven is like unto treasure hid in a field; the which when a man hath found, he hideth, and for joy thereof goeth and selleth all that he hath and buyeth that field. Again, the kingdom of heaven is like unto a merchantman seeking goodly pearls; who, when he had found one pearl of great price, went and sold all that he had and bought it." Alas! the inconveniences of this plan were not long in making themselves felt. A treasurer was wanted. They chose for that office Judas of Kerioth. Rightly or wrongly, they accused him of stealing from the common purse; it is certain that he came to a bad end.

Sometimes the master, more versed in things of heaven than those of earth, taught a still more singular political economy. In a strange parable, a steward is praised for having made himself friends among the poor at the expense of his master, in order that the poor might in their turn introduce him into the kingdom of heaven. The poor, in fact, becoming the dispensers of this kingdom, will only receive those who have given to them. A prudent man, thinking of the future, ought therefore to seek to gain their favor. "And the Pharisees also," says the evangelist, "who were covetous, heard all these things: and they derided him." Did they also hear the formidable parable which follows? "There was a certain rich man, which was clothed in purple and fine linen, and fared sumptuously every day: and there was a certain beggar named Lazarus, which was laid at his gate, full of sores, and desiring to be fed with the crumbs which fell from the rich man's table: moreover the dogs came and licked his sores. And it came to pass, that the beggar died, and was carried by the angels into Abraham's bosom: the rich man also died, and was buried; and in hell he lifted up his eyes, being in torments, and seeth Abraham afar off, and Lazarus in his bosom. And he cried and said, 'Father Abraham, have mercy on me, and send Lazarus that he may dip the tip of his finger in water, and cool my tongue; for I am tormented in this flame.' But Abraham said, 'Son, remember that thou in thy lifetime receivedst thy good things; and likewise Lazarus evil things: but now he is comforted and thou art tormented.' " What more just? Afterward this parable was called that of the "wicked rich man." But it is purely and simply the parable of the "rich man." He is in hell because he is rich, because he does not give his wealth to the poor, because he dines well, while others at his door dine badly. Lastly, in a less extravagant moment, Jesus does not make it obligatory to sell one's goods and give them to the poor except as a suggestion toward greater perfection. But he still makes this terrible declaration: "It is easier for a camel to go through the eye of a needle than for a rich man to enter into the kingdom of God."

An admirable idea governed Jesus in all this, as well as the band of joyous children who accompanied him and made him for eternity the true creator of the peace of the soul, the great consoler of life. In disengaging man from what he called "the cares of the world," Jesus might go to excess and injure the essential conditions of human society; but he founded that high spiritualism which for centuries has filled souls with joy in the midst of this vale of tears. He saw with perfect clearness that man's inattention, his want of philosophy and morality, come mostly from the distractions which he permits himself, the cares which besiege him, and which civilization multiplies beyond measure. The Gospel, in this manner, has been the most efficient remedy for the weariness of ordinary life, a perpetual *sursum corda,* a powerful diversion from the miserable cares of earth, a gentle appeal like that of Jesus in the ear of Martha—"Martha, Martha, thou art careful and troubled about many things; but one thing is needful." Thanks to Jesus, the dullest existence, that most absorbed by sad or humiliating duties, has had its glimpse of heaven. In our busy civilizations the remembrance of the free life of Galilee has been like perfume from another world, like the "dew of Hermon," which has prevented drought and barrenness from entirely invading the field of God.

JESUS THE MAN BECOME OBSESSED [3]

As Renan's account of Jesus' life unfolds, the Galilean idyll in which Jesus shared with his followers amid seas of waving corn, distant mountains, and gleaming lilies in Galilee very quickly vanishes. The gentle persuasive teacher becomes an angry denunciator, his mind gripped with apocalyptic terrors.

It is clear that such a religious society, founded solely on the expectation of the kingdom of God, must be in itself very incomplete. The first Christian generation lived almost entirely upon

[3] E. Renan, *op. cit.,* pp. 285-294.

expectations and dreams. On the eve of seeing the world come to an end, they regarded as useless everything which only served to prolong it. Possession of property was interdicted. Everything which attaches man to earth, everything which draws him aside from heaven, was to be avoided. Although several of the disciples were married, there was to be no more marriage on becoming a member of the sect. The celibate was greatly preferred; even in marriage continence was recommended. At one time the Master seems to approve of those who should mutilate themselves in prospect of the kingdom of God. In this he was consistent with his principle: "If thy hand or thy foot offend thee, cut them off, and cast them from thee; it is better for thee to enter into life halt or maimed, rather than having two hands or two feet to be cast into everlasting fire. And if thine eye offend thee, pluck it out, and cast it from thee; it is better for thee to enter into life with one eye, rather than having two eyes to be cast into hell-fire." The cessation of generation was often considered as the sign and condition of the kingdom of God.

Never, we perceive, would this primitive Church have formed a lasting society but for the great variety of germs deposited by Jesus in his teaching. It required more than a century for the true Christian Church—that which has converted the world—to disengage itself from this little sect of "latter-day saints," and to become a framework applicable to the whole of human society. The same thing, indeed, took place in Buddhism, which at first was founded only for monks. The same thing would have happened in the order of St. Francis if that order had succeeded in its society. Essentially Utopian in their origin, and succeeding by their very exaggeration, the great systems of which we have just spoken have only laid hold of the world by being profoundly modified, and by abandoning their excesses. Jesus did not advance beyond this first and entirely monachal period, in which it was believed that the impossible could be attempted with impunity. He made no concession to necessity. He boldly preached war against nature, and total severance from ties of blood. "Verily I say unto you," said he, "there is no man that hath left house, or parents, or brethren, or wife, or children, for the kingdom of God's sake, who shall not receive manifold more in this present time, and in the world to come life everlasting."

The teachings which Jesus is reputed to have given to his disciples breathe the same exaltation. He who was so tolerant to the world outside, he who contented himself sometimes with half adhesions, exercised toward his own an extreme rigor. He would have no "all buts." We should call it an "order," constituted by the most austere rules. Faithful to his idea that the cares of life trouble man, and draw him downward, Jesus required from his associates a complete detachment from the earth, an absolute devotion to his work. They were not to carry with them either money or provisions for the way, not even a scrip, or change of raiment. They must practise absolute poverty, live on alms and hospitality. "Freely ye have received, freely give," said he, in his beautiful language. Arrested and arraigned before the judges, they were not to prepare their defence; the *Peraklit,* the heavenly advocate, would inspire them with what they ought to say. The Father would send them his Spirit from on high, which would become the principle of all their acts, the director of their thoughts, and their guide through the world. If driven from any town, they were to shake the dust from their shoes, declaring always the proximity of the kingdom of God, that none might plead ignorance. "Ye shall not have gone over the cities of Israel," added he, "till the Son of man be come."

A strange ardor animates all these discourses, which may in part be the creation of the enthusiasm of his disciples, but which even in that case came indirectly from Jesus, for it was he who had inspired the enthusiasm. He predicted for his followers severe persecutions and the hatred of mankind. He sent them forth as lambs in the midst of wolves. They would be scourged in the synagogues, and dragged to prison. Brother should deliver up brother to death, and the father his son. When they were persecuted in one country they were to flee to another. "The disciple," said he, "is not above his master, nor the servant above his lord. Fear not them which kill the body, but are not able to kill the soul. Are not two sparrows sold for a farthing? and one of them shall not fall to the ground without your Father. But the very hairs of your head are all numbered. Fear ye not, therefore, ye are of more value than many sparrows." "Whosoever, therefore," continued he, "shall confess me before men, him will I confess also before my Father which is in heaven. But whosoever shall deny me before men, him will I also deny before my Father which is in heaven."

In these fits of severity he went so far as to abolish all natural ties. His requirements had no longer any bounds. Despising the healthy limits of man's nature, he demanded that he should exist only for him, that he should love him alone. "If any man come to me," said he, "and hate not his father, and mother, and wife, and children, and brethren, and sisters, and his own life also, he cannot be my disciple." "So likewise, whosoever he be of you that forsaketh not all that he hath, he cannot be my disciple." There was, at such times, something strange and more than human in his words; they were like a fire utterly consuming life, and reducing everything to a frightful wilderness. The harsh and gloomy feeling of distaste for the world, and of excessive self-abnegation which characterizes Christian perfection, was originated, not by the refined and cheerful moralist of earlier days, but by the sombre giant whom a kind of grand presentiment was withdrawing, more and more, out of the pale of humanity. We should almost say that, in these moments of conflict with the most legitimate cravings of the heart, Jesus had forgotten the pleasure of living, of loving, of seeing, and of feeling. Employing still more unmeasured language, he even said, "If any man will come after me, let him deny himself and follow me. He that loveth father or mother more than me, is not worthy of me; and he that loveth son or daughter more than me, is not worthy of me. He that findeth his life shall lose it, and he that loseth his life for my sake and the gospel's, shall find it. What is a man profited if he shall gain the whole world, and lose his own soul?" Two anecdotes of the kind we cannot accept as historical, but which, although they were exaggerations, were intended to represent a characteristic feature, clearly illustrate this defiance of nature. He said to one man, "Follow me!"—But he said, "Lord, suffer me first to go and bury my father." Jesus answered, "Let the dead bury their dead: but go thou and preach the kingdom of God." Another said to him, "Lord, I will follow thee; but let me first go bid them farewell, which are at home at my house." Jesus replied, "No man, having put his hand to the plough, and looking back, is fit for the kingdom of God." An extraordinary confidence, and at times accents of singular sweetness, reversing all our ideas of him, caused these exaggerations to be easily received. "Come unto me," cried he, "all ye that labor and are heavy laden, and I will give you rest. Take my yoke upon you, and learn of me: for I am meek and lowly in heart: and ye shall find rest unto your souls. For my yoke is easy, and my burden is light."

A great danger threatened the future of this exalted morality, thus expressed in hyperbolical language and with a terrible energy.

By detaching man from earth the ties of life were severed. The Christian would be praised for being a bad son, or a bad patriot, if it was for Christ that he resisted his father and fought against his country. The ancient city, the parent republic, the state, or the law common to all, were thus placed in hostility with the kingdom of God. A fatal germ of theocracy was introduced into the world.

From this point, another consequence may be perceived. This morality, created for a temporary crisis, when introduced into a peaceful country, and in the midst of a society assured of its own duration, must seem impossible. The Gospel was thus destined to become a Utopia for Christians, which few would care to realize. These terrible maxims would, for the greater number, remain in profound oblivion, an oblivion encouraged by the clergy itself; the Gospel man would prove a dangerous man. The most selfish, proud, hard and worldly of all human beings, a Louis XIV, for instance, would find priests to persuade him, in spite of the Gospel, that he was a Christian. But, on the other hand, there would always be found holy men who would take the sublime paradoxes of Jesus literally. Perfection being placed beyond the ordinary conditions of society, and a complete Gospel life being only possible away from the world, the principle of asceticism and of monasticism was established. Christian societies would have two moral rules; the one moderately heroic for common men, the other exalted in the extreme for the perfect man; and the perfect man would be the monk, subjected to rules which professed to realize the Gospel ideal. It is certain that this ideal, if only on account of the celibacy and poverty it imposed, could not become the common law. The monk would be thus, in one sense, the only true Christian. Common sense revolts at these excesses; and if we are guided by it, to demand the impossible, is a mark of weakness and error. But common sense is a bad judge where great matters are in question. To obtain little from humanity we must ask much. The immense moral progress which we owe to the Gospel is the result of its exaggerations. It is thus that it has been, like stoicism, but with infinitely greater fulness, a living argument for the divine powers in man, an exalted monument of the potency of the will.

We may easily imagine that to Jesus, at this period of his life, everything which was not the kingdom of God had absolutely disappeared. He was, if we may say so, totally outside nature: family, friendship, country, had no longer any meaning for him. No doubt from this moment he had already sacrificed his life. Sometimes we are tempted to believe that, seeing in his own death a means of founding his kingdom, he deliberately determined to allow himself to be killed. At other times, although such a thought only afterward became a doctrine, death presented itself to him as a sacrifice, destined to appease his Father and to save mankind. A singular taste for persecution and torments possessed him. His blood appeared to him as the water of a second baptism with which he ought to be baptized, and he seemed possessed by a strange haste to anticipate this baptism, which alone could quench his thirst.

The grandeur of his views upon the future was at times surprising. He did not conceal from himself the terrible storm he was about to cause in the world. "Think not," said he, with much boldness and beauty, "that I am come to send peace on earth: I came not to send peace, but a sword. There shall be five in one house divided, three against two, and two against three. I am come to set a man at variance against his father, and the daughter against her mother, and the daughter-in-law against her mother-in-law. And a man's foes shall be they of his own household." "I am come to send fire on the earth; and what will I, if it be already kindled?" "They shall put you out of the synagogues," he continued; "yea, the time cometh, that whosoever killeth you, will think that he doeth God service." "If the world hate you, ye know that it hated me before it hated you. Remember the word that I said unto you: The servant is not greater than his lord. If they have persecuted me, they will also persecute you."

Carried away by this fearful progression of enthusiasm, and governed by the necessities of a preaching becoming daily more exalted, Jesus was no longer free; he belonged to his mission, and, in one sense, to mankind. Sometimes one would have said that his reason was disturbed. He suffered great mental anguish and agitation. The great vision of the kingdom of God, glistening before his eyes, bewildered him. His disciples at times thought him mad. His enemies declared him to be possessed. His excessively impassioned temperament carried him incessantly beyond the bounds of human nature. He laughed at all human systems, and his work not being a work of the reason, that which he most imperiously required was "faith." This was the word most frequently repeated in the little guest-chamber. It is the watchword of all popular movements. It is clear that none of these movements would take place if it were necessary that their author should gain his disciples one by one by force of logic. Reflection leads only to doubt. If the authors of the French Revolution, for instance, had had to be previously convinced by lengthened meditations, they would all have become old without accomplishing anything; Jesus, in like manner, aimed less at convincing his hearers than at exciting their enthusiasm. Urgent and imperative, he suffered no opposition: men must be converted, nothing less would satisfy him. His natural gentleness seemed to have abandoned him; he was sometimes harsh and capricious. His disciples at times did not understand him, and experienced in his presence a feeling akin to fear. Sometimes his displeasure at the slightest opposition led him to commit inexplicable and apparently absurd acts.

It was not that his virtue deteriorated; but his struggle for the ideal against the reality became insupportable. Contact with the world pained and revolted him. Obstacles irritated him. His idea of the Son of God became disturbed and exaggerated. The fatal law which condemns an idea to decay as soon as it seeks to convert men applied to him. Contact with men degraded him to their level. The tone he had adopted could not be sustained more than a few months; it was time that death came to liberate him from an endurance strained to the utmost, to remove him from the impossibilities of an interminable path, and by delivering him from a trial in danger of being too prolonged, introduce him henceforth sinless into celestial peace.

THE LAZARUS EPISODE AT BETHANY [4]

A fair number of scholars would now agree that the account of the raising of Lazarus in John 11:1ff. is to be taken as an edifying legend. Renan has his own very different explanation, as the following extract shows—Jesus obsessed stoops to fraudulent practice.

After Jesus had completed this kind of pilgrimage to the scenes of his earliest prophetic activity, he returned to his beloved

[4] E. Renan, *op. cit.*, pp. 321-324.

abode in Bethany, where a singular event occurred, which seems to have had a powerful influence on the remaining days of his life. Tired of the cold reception which the kingdom of God found in the capital, the friends of Jesus wished for a great miracle which should strike powerfuly the incredulity of the Hierosolymites. The resurrection of a man known at Jerusalem appeared to them most likely to carry conviction. We must bear in mind that the essential condition of true criticism is to understand the diversity of times, and to rid ourselves of the instinctive repugnances which are the fruit of a purely rational education. We must also remember that in this dull and impure city of Jerusalem Jesus was no longer himself. Not by any fault of his own, but by that of others, his conscience had lost something of its original purity. Desperate, and driven to extremity, he was no longer his own master. His mission overwhelmed him, and he yielded to the torrent. As always happens in the lives of great and inspired men, he suffered the miracles opinion demanded of him rather than performed them. At this distance of time, and with only a single text, bearing evident traces of artifices of composition, it is impossible to decide whether in this instance the whole is fiction, or whether a real fact which happened at Bethany has served as basis to the rumours which were spread about it. It must be acknowledged, however, that the way John narrates the incident differs widely from those descriptions of miracles, the offspring of the popular imagination, which fill the Synoptics. Let us add that John is the only evangelist who has a precise knowledge of the relations of Jesus with the family of Bethany, and that it is impossible to believe that a mere creation of the popular mind could exist in a collection of remembrances so entirely personal. It is, then, probable that the miracle in question was not one of those purely legendary ones for which no one is responsible. In other words, we think that something really happened at Bethany which was looked upon as a resurrection.

Fame already attributed to Jesus two or three works of this kind. The family of Bethany might be led, almost without suspecting it, into taking part in the important act which was desired. Jesus was adored by them. It seems that Lazarus was sick, and that in consequence of receiving a message from the anxious sisters Jesus left Perea. They thought that the joy Lazarus would feel at his arrival might restore him to life. Perhaps, also, the ardent desire of silencing those who violently denied the divine mission of Jesus carried his enthusiastic friends beyond all bounds. It may be that Lazarus, still pallid with disease, caused himself to be wrapped in bandages as if dead, and shut up in the tomb of his family. These tombs were large vaults cut in the rock, and were entered by a square opening, closed by an enormous stone. Martha and Mary went to meet Jesus, and, without allowing him to enter Bethany, conducted him to the cave. The emotion which Jesus experienced at the tomb of his friend, whom he believed to be dead, might be taken by those present for the agitation and trembling which accompanied miracles. Popular opinion required that the divine virtue should manifest itself in man as an epileptic and convulsive principle. Jesus (if we follow the above hypothesis) desired to see once more him whom he had loved; and, the stone being removed, Lazarus came forth in his bandages, his head covered with a winding-sheet. This reappearance would naturally be regarded by everyone as a resurrection. Faith knows no other law than the interest of that which it believes to be true. Regarding the object which it pursues as absolutely holy, it makes no scruple of invoking bad arguments in support of its thesis when good ones do not succeed. If such and such a proof be not sound, many others are! If such and such a wonder be not real, many others have been! Being intimately persuaded that Jesus was a thaumaturgus, Lazarus and his two sisters may have aided in the execution of one of his miracles, just as many pious men who, convinced of the truth of their religion, have sought to triumph over the obstinacy of their opponents by means of whose weakness they are well aware. The state of their conscience was that of the stigmatists, of the convulsionists, of the possessed ones in convents, drawn, by the influence of the world in which they live, and by their own belief, into feigned acts. As to Jesus, he was no more able than St. Bernard or St. Francis d'Assisi to moderate the avidity for the marvellous displayed by the multitude, and even by his own disciples. Death, moreover, in a few days would restore him his divine liberty, and release him from the fatal necessities of a position which each day became more exacting and more difficult to sustain.

Everything, in fact, seems to lead us to believe that the miracle of Bethany contributed sensibly to hasten the death of Jesus. The persons who had been witnesses of it were dispersed throughout the city, and spoke much about it. The disciples related the fact, with details as to its performance, prepared in expectation of controversy.

NOSTALGIA IN THE GARDEN OF GETHSEMANE[5]

Renan never married. The woman in his life was his sister, Henriette, to whom he remained ever devoted. Not a few of his remarks on Jesus are weakly sentimental and reveal an apparent streak of effeminacy in his character. Among such remarks are his suggestion that during his moments of agony in Gethsemane Jesus' mind may have turned to the maidens he had wooed in Galilee. One young Frenchwoman who had just finished reading the Vie de Jésus *is reported to have put it down with the comment: "What a pity it does not end with a marriage!"*

A deep melancholy appears, during these last days, to have filled the soul of Jesus, who was generally so joyous and serene. All the narratives agree in relating that before his arrest he underwent a short experience of doubt and trouble; a kind of anticipated agony. According to some, he suddenly exclaimed, "Now is my soul troubled. O Father, save me from this hour." It was believed that a voice from heaven was heard at this moment: others said that an angel came to console him. According to one widely-spread version, the incident took place in the garden of Gethsemane. Jesus, it was said, went about a stone's throw from his sleeping disciples, taking with him only Peter and the two sons of Zebedee, and fell on his face and prayed. His soul was sad even unto death; a terrible anguish weighed upon him; but resignation to the Divine will sustained him. This scene, owing to the instinctive art which regulated the compilation of the Synoptics, and often led them in the arrangement of the narrative to study adaptability and effect, has been given as occurring on the last night of the life of Jesus, and at the precise moment of his arrest. If this version were the true one, we should scarcely understand why John, who had been the intimate witness of so touching an episode, should not mention it in the very circumstantial narrative which he has furnished of the evening of

[5] E. Renan, *op. cit.*, pp. 333-336.

the Thursday. All that we can safely say is, that during his last days the enormous weight of the mission he had accepted pressed cruelly upon Jesus. Human nature asserted itself for a time. Perhaps he began to hesitate about his work. Terror and doubt took possession of him, and threw him into a state of exhaustion worse than death. He who has sacrificed his repose and the legitimate rewards of life to a great idea always experiences a feeling of revulsion when the image of death presents itself to him for the first time, and seeks to persuade him that all has been in vain. Perhaps some of those touching reminiscences which the strongest souls preserve, and which at times pierce like a sword, came upon him at this moment. Did he remember the clear fountains of Galilee where he was wont to refresh himself: the vine and the fig-tree under which he had reposed, and the young maidens who, perhaps, would have consented to love him? Did he curse the hard destiny which had denied him the joys conceded to all others? Did he regret his too lofty nature, and, victim of his greatness, did he mourn that he had not remained a simple artisan of Nazareth? We know not. For all these internal troubles evidently were a sealed letter to his disciples. They understood nothing of them, and supplied by simple conjectures that which in the great soul of their Master was obscure to them. It is certain at least that his Divine nature soon regained the supremacy. He might still have avoided death; but he would not. Love for his work sustained him. He was willing to drink the cup to the dregs. Henceforth we behold Jesus entirely himself; his character unclouded. The subtleties of the polemic, the credulity of the thaumaturgus and of the exorcist, are forgotten. There remains only the incomparable hero of the Passion, the founder of the rights of the free conscience, and the complete model which all suffering souls will contemplate in order to fortify and console themselves.

PANEGYRIC ON JESUS [6]

This sublime person, who each day still presides over the destiny of the world, we may call divine, not in the sense that Jesus has absorbed all the divine, or has been adequate to it (to employ an expression of the schoolmen), but in the sense that Jesus is the one who has caused his fellow-men to make the greatest step towards

[6] E. Renan, *op. cit.*, pp. 392-393.

the divine. Mankind in its totality offers an assemblage of low beings, selfish, and superior to the animal only in that its selfishness is more reflective. From the midst of this uniform mediocrity there are pillars that rise towards the sky, and bear witness to a nobler destiny. Jesus is the highest of these pillars which show to man whence he comes, and whither he ought to tend. In him was condensed all that is good and elevated in our nature. He was not sinless; he has conquered the same passions that we combat; no angel of God comforted him, except his good conscience; no Satan tempted him, except that which each one bears in his heart. In the same way that many of his great qualities are lost to us, through the fault of his disciples, it is also probable that many of his faults have been concealed. But never has any one so much as he made the interests of humanity predominate in his life over the littlenesses of self-love. Unreservedly devoted to his mission, he subordinated everything to it to such a degree that towards the end of his life the universe no longer existed for him. It was by this access of heroic will that he conquered heaven. There never was a man, Cakya-Mouni perhaps excepted, who has to this degree trampled under foot family, the joys of this world, and all temporal care. Jesus only lived for his Father and the divine mission which he believed himself destined to fulfil.

As to us, eternal children, powerless as we are, we who labour without reaping, and who will never see the fruit of that which we have sown, let us bow before these demi-gods. They were able to do that which we cannot do: to create, to affirm, to act. Will great originality be born again, or will the world content itself henceforth by following the ways opened by the bold creators of the ancient ages? We know not. But whatever may be the unexpected phenomena of the future, Jesus will not be surpassed. His worship will constantly renew its youth, the tale of his life will cause ceaseless tears, his sufferings will soften the best hearts; all the ages will proclaim that among the sons of men there is none born who is greater than Jesus.

There is an obvious inconsistency between Renan's concluding eloquent tribute to Jesus (a vestige of his Catholic upbringing?) and his earlier picture of the obsessed visionary who even stoops to fraud. There are other inconsistencies. Renan plays a nice game of chess with episodes and sayings in the Gospels, moving them around at will to suit his predetermined plan and pattern. Happy incidents from the later tragic part of Jesus' ministry he transposes to the joyous earlier days. Conversely any untoward incident in the earlier good days, like that of Jesus' mother seeking him in the belief that he is beside himself, he transposes to the gloomy later time. The weakness of his work? Simply, according to Schweitzer, that "it is written by one to whom the New Testament was to the last something foreign, who had not read it from his youth up in the mother-tongue, who was not accustomed to breathe freely in its simple and pure world, but must perfume it with sentimentality in order to feel himself at home in it." [7]

[7] Schweitzer, *The Quest of the Historical Jesus,* p. 192.

5

D. F. Strauss: Myth and History

From Germany, D. F. Strauss "shook hands with Renan across the Rhine." Just when Renan's Vie de Jésus *appeared, David Friedrich Strauss was busy completing his work on* The Life of Jesus for the People. *It was in fact published at Leipzig in 1864.*

Twenty-nine years previously he had aimed an earlier Life of Jesus at the theologians, to the great chagrin of many of them. Strauss's whole career was in fact marred by a series of violent upheavals. Acrimonious critics among the theologians dogged his steps all the way. "He had a prophet's fate. Disappointment and suffering gave his life its consecration. It unrolls itself before us like a tragedy." His first Life of Jesus suffered in Germany the same fate as did Sir John Seely's famous book on the human Jesus, Ecce Homo, *in England—it was cursed by religious readers as "the most pestilential book ever vomited out of the jaws of hell."*

Yet the book was far more than merely an attack on the miraculous or supernatural element in the Gospels. Dissatisfied as much with the rationalistic as with the supernaturalistic explanation of events in Jesus' life, under the aegis of the Hegelian philosophy of history Strauss sought a synthesis in his own mythological interpretation. There was good reason why he was able to press the conception of myth in the Gospel narratives with greater fearlessness and consistency than his predecessors. He was convinced that there was something in the Gospels that criticism could never touch, far less destroy—the Idea *of God-manhood embodied in the life and person of Jesus, and thereby made real to humanity as the ultimate goal of mankind.*

Even so this first Life did contain several fresh ideas on the historical Jesus that marked Strauss out as in some respects ahead of his time. For instance, he emphasized the centrality of the supernatural realization of the kingdom of God in Jesus' message and defended the authenticity of Jesus' claim that in the coming kingdom he would be manifested as the Son of Man.

The later Life for the People *shows a decline of nerve and verve on Strauss's part. Unceasing pressures from his enemies led to his making concessions. The preface betrays his sensitivity to the hostility of the clerical caste and his ambition to reach the people instead.*

A LIFE FOR THE LAITY [1]

In the Preface to the First Edition of my former Life of Jesus, written now twenty-nine years ago, I particularly mentioned that the work was intended for theologians; that for others no adequate preparation had been made, so that the book was purposely thrown into a form unsuited for lay comprehension. On the present occasion I write especially for the use of laymen, and have taken particular pains that no single sentence shall be unintelligible to any educated or thoughtful person; whether professional theologians also choose to be among my readers is to me a matter of indifference.

So greatly have things changed during the interval! The general public can now no longer be considered unprepared for inquiries of this nature. Independently of any act of mine, these questions were rashly thrown before the multitude by my bitterest adversaries, the very men who insisted that, in decency, I ought at least to have written in Latin. The loud outcries of these advocates of caution were repeated by persons less scrupulous than myself, and treated in a popular, though to me not very palatable form; until at length the political resuscitation of Germany opened a freer platform for religious as well as other discussions. In consequence of this, many minds have become unsettled in their attachment to old ideas, and roused to independent thought upon religious subjects; while at the same time a variety of preliminary conceptions, which could not be reckoned on as familiar at the time of the publication of my first work, have since become popularly current. Moreover, it is a mere prejudice of caste to fancy that ability to comprehend these things appertains exclusively to the theologian or man of learning. On the contrary, the essence of the matter is so

[1] D. F. Strauss, *The Life of Jesus for the People* (London and Edinburgh: Williams and Norgate, 1874), I, vii-viii. All selections reprinted by permission of Ernest Benn Limited.

simple, that every one whose head and heart are in the right place may well rest assured that whatever, after due reflection and the proper use of accessible means, still remains incomprehensible to him, is in itself of very little value.

Again, the interval has made it perfectly clear that professional theologians are precisely those from whom an unprejudiced judgment in these matters is least to be expected. They are in fact interested parties adjudicating their own cause. Any discussion as to the objects of Christian faith as traditionally given, especially as to the Gospel records which are its basis, seems to imply a doubt as to the propriety of the estimation in which they are held as spiritual leaders. Whether rightly or wrongly is immaterial; such they believe to be the case. And to every class or caste its own stability is the first consideration; few indeed among its members would encourage innovations menacing its own safety. And clearly, so soon as Christianity ceases to be thought miraculous, the clergy must cease to seem the miraculously gifted persons they have hitherto represented themselves. Their business will rather be to teach than to confer benedictions, and every one knows that the former office is as difficult and thankless as the latter is remunerative and easy.

At the close of his preface, Strauss expresses the hope that he may have written "a book as suitable for Germany as Renan's is for France." It is hardly so! it lacks the color of Renan's vivid biographical picture and can scarcely be called a "life" at all, so great is the space given to the course of Gospel criticism up to Strauss's time. But let the reader judge from the following excerpts. The first is from Volume I, in which Strauss attempts to sift out the historical from the unhistorical data about Jesus. The second is from Volume II, in which Strauss traces the rise and growth of the "mythical history of Jesus."

"THE RELIGIOUS CONSCIOUSNESS OF JESUS" [2]

Now if we would learn what, independent of the national idea of the Messiah, the peculiar religious consciousness of Jesus

[2] D. F. Strauss, *op. cit.*, I, 270-274.

was, we are referred, not only by the traditional view of the Church, but also by the theological tendency now prevailing, principally to the Gospel of John, in which the disciple who lay on the bosom of Jesus described the inmost secrets, as it were, of this bosom, the most profound revelations of Jesus about his own nature and his relation to God. On this point the old theology went fairly and freely to work, taking the bull by the horns, and explaining all that Jesus in the fourth Gospel says of himself, as the only begotten Son of God, as the light of the world, as him who is in the Father, and in whom mankind sees the Father, who came down from heaven and returns to heaven, simply from what is plainly stated in the same Gospel, partly as the doctrine of the Evangelist, partly also as the testimony of Jesus about himself, namely, that he, as the personal, divine creative Word, had been from eternity with God; had then for a time, for the purposes of the redemption of mankind, become man, in order, when he had fulfilled this object, again to return to God in heaven (i. 1ff., xiv. 3, xiii. 16, vi. 62, viii. 58, xvii. 5). According to this, then, the self-consciousness of Jesus would have been that of a divine Being, who adopted, only transiently, a human body, perhaps also a human soul, and in doing so preserved a distinct recollection of his earlier condition, the full consciousness of his divinity. Even the dependence on the Father, in which this Johannine Jesus felt himself to be, was not that of a human being on the Divine, but that of the creative subordinate God on God in the highest sense.

With a Jesus of this character, who for the theology of the ancient faith was precisely the one it required, that of the modern faith will have nothing more to do, and inasmuch as it is in its favourite Gospel that this Jesus is found in the most unmistakeable manner, it is in a difficulty. "The moment," says Schleiermacher in his Lectures upon the Life of Jesus, "that we allow the consciousness of a pre-existence in Jesus to be considered an actual recollection, the really human consciousness in him ceases." Consequently what Jesus in the Johannine Gospel says in this sense, must not be taken literally; there is implied in it, not a recollection, but only the assumption, that the Divine counsels, even from the first, pointed to him as the Redeemer. But when a Gospel begins with the propositions, that in the beginning was the Word, with God, and itself God, that by this was the world created, and that it subsequently became flesh in Jesus; and then this Jesus appears assuring us that he was before Abraham, and speaks of the glory which, before the world was, he had with God—then we hear the Eternal creative Word speaking plainly in the flesh, and remembering his personal existence before the creation of man, and we shall reject every other explanation of his words as garbled and untrue, like those of which the palliative theology of the present day is continually producing instances.

It is indeed inconceivable to us that any person in the flesh should remember an ante-natal existence, even independent of the fact that in the present case it is supposed to have been a divine existence reaching back to a period before the creation of the world. It is inconceivable to us, because in accredited history no instance of it has occurred. And if any one should speak of having such a recollection, we should consider him a fool, or, if not, an imposter. Now it is as difficult to believe that Jesus was either of these, in the presence of the effects which he produced, and of the speeches and acts the accounts of which are preserved to us in more credible records, as it is easy—nay, as has been indicated to us by all that has gone before—to assume that the fourth Evangelist is here making Jesus speak on the principles of the Alexandrian system. We do not therefore grudge these words their full literal meaning, any more than we allow ourselves to suppose that they were really spoken by Jesus.

But, even independent of any reference to an alleged pre-existence, the utterances of Jesus about himself in the fourth Gospel are of a kind which makes it difficult, from them, to imagine what his personal self-consciousness can have been.[3] Whether a God, having become man, would do as the Johannine Jesus does; whether in his speeches he would so strongly and incessantly insist upon his divinity, and be so continually challenging afresh the contradiction

[3] The problem of what contribution, if any, the Gospel of John has to make to the study of the life of Jesus was much debated in the nineteenth century. It has continued to preoccupy scholars in the present century. The consensus is still that as evidence for the actual history of Jesus the Fourth Gospel is not on a par with the Synoptics, although lately some scholars have argued for an earlier dating than the usual one (around A.D. 100), or have sought to show that the writer had access to a historical tradition independent of the Synoptics and that the evidential value of this tradition needs to be reassessed. See particularly C. H. Dodd, *Historical Tradition in the Fourth Gospel* (Cambridge, 1963). Certain affinities between the Fourth Gospel and ideas expressed by the Qumrân sect have also led to new lines of questioning [Ed.].

of men; to whom a divine first person speaking out of human lips is intolerable; whether a God, become human, would not find it wiser and more becoming to let his divinity shine forth more indirectly by the glorification of his humanity—about all this nothing definite can be said, as the assumption belongs solely to the province of the imagination. But a man, whoever he may have been, could never, if his heart and head were sound, have uttered such speeches about himself as are put into the mouth of Jesus in the fourth Gospel, even independently of those salient points which reach over into an eternity existing before time. The speeches of Jesus about himself in this Gospel are an uninterrupted Doxology, only translated out of the second person into the first, from the form of address to another, into the utterance about a self; and the fact that they are found edifying even at the present day, can only be explained by the habit of transposing them into the second person. When an enthusiastic Christian calls his Master, supposed to have been raised to heaven, the light of the world, when he says of him that he who has seen him has seen the Father, that is God himself, we excuse the faithful worshipper such extravagances. But when he goes so far as the fourth Evangelist, and puts the utterances of his own pious enthusiasm into the mouth of Jesus in the form of his own utterances about himself, he does him a very perilous service.

Every one finds the well-known expression, *l'état c'est moi,* revolting, because it claims for one man exclusively what belongs to all. In this particular case indeed there is the additional consideration that the vain prince, resting only upon appearance and show, who uttered that expression, was in no respect justified in looking upon himself as the embodiment of the state which he governed. But let us suppose a man with more right to say this, a Frederick or a Washington, even from the mouth of either of them we should be sorry to hear such an expression, or rather we feel certain that it would never occur to a man of this description to speak in this way. The saying that the King is only the head-servant of the State, is as honourable to Frederick the Great as that proud expression is disgraceful to Louis XIV. We think that the former knew too well what the State is, and what, in relation to it, even the most highly-placed individual is, to presume himself alone to represent the State. To such a character Jesus corresponds when he modestly says, "Why callest thou me good? No one is good but God alone" (Mark x. 18; Luke xvii. 19). And as we honour him for this, so the sayings put into his mouth by John, "He who sees me sees the Father" (xiv. 9), or, "I and my Father are one," are offensive to us, or at any rate incomprehensible. We think (looking at the case exclusively in a human point of view, as we are here doing) that let a man have been ever so vividly conscious of representing in himself the utmost perfection of the idea of religion, the reconciliation of human self-consciousness with Divine self-consciousness, still he will ever remember, and the more in proportion to the fineness of his religious feeling, that there is between the two a gulf not to be passed, and he will hesitate the less to declare this, the better he understands what serves to awaken among men a genuine piety. No man of true religious feeling could ever have uttered the expression, "Who sees me, sees the Father"; but it is very possible that an enthusiastic worshipper of a later age might have represented him as saying it, when he had accustomed himself to regard him as a subordinate God who had become man.

"SEA ANECDOTES" [4]

Strauss was the first to apply the concept of myth to the Gospels comprehensively and consistently. He felt that between the life of Jesus and the date of composition of the Gospels there was ample time for the historical materials to be mythicized. Myth, as Strauss understood it, was the process whereby religious ideas or ideals came to be expressed in concrete historical form and embodied, with the help of the inventive power of legend, in a particular historical person. The mythical in this sense, Strauss thought, permeated the Gospel traditions and not least the accounts of the transfiguration, resurrection, and ascension. The myth-making process also of course was responsible for the form in which the miracle stories have come down to us, and they must not be explained as supernatural phenomena or explained away naturalistically.

It may be added here that Strauss's near contemporary, the enigmatic and bitterly controversial Bruno Bauer, set out at first to continue the former's work except that he regarded the person of Jesus in the Gospel story not as the end result of myth and legend, but as the very embodiment of the Church's own communal experience. To Bauer's mind the temptation narrative is nothing other than the translation and applica-

[4] D. F. Strauss, *op. cit.*, II, 234-241.

tion to the person of Jesus of the Church's own inner conflict. Unlike Strauss, Bauer finished in total scepticism, having attributed so much that is said of Jesus' person in the Gospels to the Church's psyche that he raised doubt about whether Jesus ever existed at all.

As the dwelling of Jesus was situated on the Sea of Galilee, and his ministry, for the greatest part of the time, was confined to its shore, it was natural that there should be a connection between the sea and a portion of the miraculous histories circulated about him. Of these anecdotes, we may describe one-half more immediately as Fishing legends, the other as Sailing legends, in so far as the one class refers to fishing as the trade of a portion of the disciples, the other to the element of water as a means of transport. Of the anecdotes of the first class we have that of the miraculous draught of fish by Peter in Luke. Of this we have already spoken, because it is connected with his call to be a fisher of men, and we combined with it, in consequence of the internal connection, notwithstanding its occurrence at a period so much later, the draught of fishes in the supplement to the Johannine Gospel. There remains yet the history of the piece of money, which, as advised by Jesus, Peter is supposed to have found in the mouth of a fish (Matt. xvii. 24-27).

By this miraculous history, which is peculiar to Matthew, all explanations appear to be put to shame. The believers in miracles cannot answer the question when asked, where was the necessity or even the good of so strange a miracle as that of bringing to Peter's hook a fish with a piece of money in its mouth, and how, without a second miracle, the fish, when opening its mouth to snap at the hook, could still have held the coin in it. The natural explanation which represents the piece of money, not as having been found immediately in the mouth of the fish, but earned by the sale of it, offends too much against the text, which connects the finding of the coin immediately with the opening of the mouth of the fish. As the Evangelist only mentions the recommendation given by Jesus, but does not say that Peter followed it and really found a piece of gold in the mouth of the fish, there has been lately an inclination to understand the expression of Jesus merely figuratively and proverbially, as when we say of the dawn that it has gold in its mouth; but the execution of an order of Jesus, and the correspondence between a prediction of his and the result predicted, are taken in the Gospel as a matter of course. And even the mythical explanation does not appear altogether suitable to an account of a miracle which has neither the character of a fulfilment of a Messianic expectation, nor an embodiment of an original Christian conception, but of a capricious result of an uncontrolled imagination.

Meanwhile, if we examine the case more accurately, the narrative in question has the character of a miraculous history only at the conclusion. At the beginning and in the middle it looks exactly like one of those discussions, several of which are contained in the three first Gospels, and among these it has an unmistakeable connection with that about the tribute-money (Matt. xx. 15-22; Mark xii. 13-17; Luke xx. 20-26). In each case the discussion refers to a tax; in the former case, the tribute to the Romans, and the question is asked whether it is right for the Jews to pay it; in this case the tribute is for the Temple at Jerusalem, and the question is whether Jesus and his disciples are bound to pay it. In the former case, Jesus decides the question in the affirmative, after ordering the tribute-money, a denarius, to be shewn to him; in this case, after deciding the question negatively, he himself miraculously provides the tribute-money, a stater, in order to settle the matter amicably.

As the dispute as to whether the people of God were free from sin in recognising in the Romans any supreme authority besides them, had continued among the Jews since the days of Judas the Gaulonite, it is possible that a question bearing upon this dispute may have been at some time or other put to Jesus. It is, on the other hand, less probable that the question as to his obligation, and that of his followers, to pay tribute to the Temple at Jerusalem, was mooted in his lifetime. It was not until a considerable time after his death, when the Christian community had separated itself more and more from the Jewish, that the question could arise as to whether the Christians were bound to contribute to the expenses of the Temple at Jerusalem. And from the Christian point of view, the most correct answer was, that in the abstract neither the Messiah, as being greater than the Temple (Matt. xii. 6), nor his adherents as the Royal Priesthood (1 Peter ii. 9), could be amenable to the tax, but that still, for the sake of precious peace, they would not refuse to pay it; a decision which, like so many other results of later development, was attributed to Jesus himself, and very probably in direct imitation of the history of the civil tribute-money.

But now the miracle? Jesus, it was thought, was not to prejudice himself at all by that admission—by that acquiescence in the payment of a tax which the Messiah was not called upon properly to pay. While he submitted to it, he must (it was considered) at the same time shew himself raised above it; he must himself provide the token of his submission in a manner which placed him above all these relations. Thus a miracle was required in this case more than in any other.

But why especially this miracle? And as on so many other occasions, so also on this, the disciple Peter is brought forward as the spokesman. It is to him that the collectors of the tax apply with the question as to whether his Master pays the tribute to the Temple; it is he whom Jesus catechises, on entering the house, with a series of questions, which lead to the conclusion that, strictly speaking, they, as children of God, are not subject to any tax for the support of the house of God; it was with him, therefore, that the miracle was most appropriately connected, which was to put into its proper light the discharge of this claim on the part of Jesus and his followers. Peter, in the original Christian tradition, was the fisherman. He had been, before all, called away from his net to undertake the office of a fisher of men; it was to him that the rich draught of fishes was vouchsafed as a type of his apostolical ministry. Jesus might now again have granted him another such, which, turned into money, would have made up the amount of the Temple-tribute. But this was an unnecessary resource. On the occasion of the former miraculous draught, the case had been different: then the question had been, not about an amount of money, but about a symbol of the apostolic ministry. So in that case only ordinary fish, only in great numbers, had been caught. In this case, on the other hand, the question was about the tribute to the Temple, payable by two persons, amounting to four drachms, or a stater. As this was to be provided miraculously, why not at once in ready money? and as it was to be provided by the fisher-Apostle, why not by a fish bringing him a stater? Consequently, as on this occasion only one fish is wanted, it was not necessary for Peter to throw out his net, but only his line; and because when the fish was caught it was necessary to open its mouth in order to extract the hook, it was necessary that the fish should have the stater in its mouth. But here the narrator, while he endeavours to make matters easy for Peter, makes the task of the fish far too difficult. Since the times of Polycrates, it has often happened that fishes have swallowed treasures and kept them in their stomachs; but for a fish, and one too caught by a hook, to have kept a piece of money in its mouth together with the hook, is without example in the history of the world.

6

Jesus, Prophet of the New Social Order

Strauss's work was one of the storm centers of the continuing debate between the liberals and the orthodox in theology over the miraculous or the supernatural in the Gospels. Of course the "debunking" of the supernatural was only one side to the progress of Liberalism. There were others. Among the succession of liberal scholars who wrote Lives of Jesus after Strauss, H. J. Holtzmann, for example, so convincingly demonstrated by literary criticism the hypothesis of the priority of Mark that it subsequently became a more or less unquestioned assumption of Gospel studies. Moreover Holtzmann found in Mark's Gospel what he took to be a reliable account of the progression of Jesus' own consciousness of his vocation. In Galilee he concealed his awareness of his Messiahship from his followers until they should become more inwardly enlightened about the true character of the kingdom of God and the Messiah (over against the popular Jewish nationalistic ideas); toward the close of the Galilean ministry he let himself be known to them as the Messiah; thereafter till the end, in face of the ever stiffening opposition that confronted him, he taught them that he must be a suffering Messiah. So was Jesus pictured as one who wanted to purge the Jewish Messianic hope of its crudely nationalistic and materialistic features, or to spiritualize it by founding a community of penitents who would form a kind of advance brigade of the kingdom of God that was to come.

From another angle, under the impact of the theology of Albrecht Ritschl, the kingdom of God in the teaching of Jesus was also understood as a distant social goal that could at last be attained by increasing moral heroism on the part of men.

In the later years of the nineteenth century, societal views of the kingdom of God associated with German Liberalism proved no less congenial to American theologians of liberal spirit, who were still very close to the frontier experience, to the constant pushing out of the boundaries and the dream of the coming great society, and who were dedicated to the cause of the "social gospel." Among the American Liberals was the Professor of New Testament History and Interpretation in the University of Chicago, Shailer Mathews. His book on The Social Teaching of Jesus *first published in 1897 wielded a considerable influence. Mathews was well aware that it is quite misleading to import back into the life and teaching of Jesus modern ideas of the "class struggle" or "social idealism."*

Jesus' chief purpose was to convert individuals to genuine spirituality. Nevertheless his teaching had the profoundest social implications inasmuch as he envisaged the kingdom of God upon earth as a distant goal at which this spirituality would manifest itself in the true brotherly love of the ideal society.

SHAILER MATHEWS: "JESUS' PHILOSOPHY OF SOCIAL PROGRESS" [1]

And here, as the outgrowth of this central thought of his system, we find a second element in Jesus' philosophy of social progress; *the love that springs from a sense of brotherhood.* Two men, brothers in the physical sense, love each other instinctively, spontaneously. So in the case of this new fraternity, of this genetic relationship that exists between two men and God. If each is a son of God, are they not brothers? If once they realize their common nature, will they not love one another? So at any rate thought Jesus. Love between a man and his enemy was a thing to be commanded, but not between brothers. That was to be expected. Anything that prevented such fraternal feeling was to be removed, even at the cost of religious punctuality. It is true that if men fail to appreciate their fraternal relations when they exist, they will need the command to love one another. But this, like all law, is but a provisional matter. As the realization of their relations to one another as members of a fraternity deepens, men will love less and less from a sense of duty

[1] Shailer Mathews, *The Social Teaching of Jesus, An Essay in Christian Sociology* (New York: The Macmillan Company, 1897), pp. 191-197. Reprinted by permission of the estate of S. Mathews.

and increasingly from impulse. And this new love was to be like Jesus' own, ready for any sacrifice that might seem necessary.

But evidently at this point we are dealing with social motives. A man thus inspired is no longer living for his individual, his atomistic self, but for his social, his altruistic self. In his revelation of the love of God and the possibility of a new and divine sonship, Jesus prepared the way not only for the saving of each individual sinner. He did more. Every man who comes thus into a conscious reinstatement in the love of God, becomes also a brother of all other men in the same relation. And so is set in motion a multitude of fraternal loves which, disregarding place, and time, and birth, and social station, will forever remain unsatisfied until they express themselves in reciprocal deeds of kindness and bring in a new social order, in which each man will seek to minister, not to be ministered unto; to become a servant of all.

If now we look somewhat more closely at this new social force which is the dynamic side of the apprehension of brotherhood (which it must not be forgotten is itself the outcome of the new and divine life in man), it will be evident that it is in itself composed of something more than mere emotional elements, and that Jesus regarded it as involving to an equal extent the will. Were it otherwise it would be impossible to see how one whose love was thus the outgrowth of the sense of a new reality could ever be expected to love a person in whose case the reality was not appreciable. Such a love, it would be urged, is perhaps understandable in the case of two persons who answer Jesus' conception of brothers, but would be inconceivable between one man who was a member of the kingdom, and another man who was not. How then could there be progress, or how could the kingdom fail to become a close corporation? But if the full sweep of Jesus' teaching be considered, it will be seen that this spontaneous love that arises from the sense of kinship may be directed towards one's enemies. It may, perhaps, not always be possible for one to feel the affection for one's opponents that seems to have been felt by Jesus, but one can always treat one's enemies *as if* they were brothers. In such a case the conduct inspired by loving affection outlines the way for duty. The same kindness that was done spontaneously for a lover is now to be done from the sense of obligation for a persecutor.

And what will these acts be? Jesus does not specifically bid the member of the kingdom to do much else than pray for and bless those who are planning his harm; but after all his meaning is not hard to find. Both the spontaneous love and the controlled love will seek the accomplishment of those conditions which go to make up Jesus' ideal society. Circumstances will naturally determine different means and different processes, but the love that springs from a sense of brotherhood, will never be satisfied until it has established a social order in which fraternity will characterize all phases of social life. Sometimes such impulse and duty will need instruction, and this, it has appeared, Jesus has given in broad principles; but in special cases, he seemed to believe that the divine life within man thus enlightened could be trusted to work out better and more Christian social institutions.

Therefore it has been that those times and places in which men have come most under the influence of the words and life of Jesus have been those in which institutions at variance with fraternity—branding, polygamy, the exposure of children, slavery, drunkenness, and licentiousness—have disappeared. Indeed, one might almost say, that there has been no healthy progress towards fraternity except as it has sprung from the sense of this divine kinship. Pleas and battles for justice have wrought revolutions and wrecked institutions; but only when they have been supplemented and corrected by this fraternal impulse have they yielded the peaceable fruits of righteousness.

Thus Jesus is thoroughly consistent with himself. The new social order which he outlines is not beyond the powers of man as he conceives them. It is true that a moral regeneration of the individual is presupposed before society as such can be perfected, but here Jesus is true to human capacities. Religion, just as much as selfish calculation, is one of the motive forces in human life, and to disregard it is to throw away the most powerful source of moral impulse. Therefore it is that while one may perhaps wonder that Jesus should have counted to so small a degree upon other forces that have made forward movements successful, it is quite impossible to say that he has erred in thus centring attention upon the religious side of man's nature and upon that enthusiasm for humanity which is the outgrowth of a perception of the consequent new human fraternity. Life is indeed something more than search for creature comforts. Those men of the past who have marked stages in the march of the race have always so judged. Take from the goodly company of the men who have permanently benefited society, those men whose impulses have not in some way sprung from the sense of God or the sense of fraternity, and how many will be left? In his revelation of divine sonship and the consequent human brotherhood, Jesus has furnished the basis for lasting social progress. For if humanity is to become a family inspired by the love of the divine Father, there is no power in earth or hell that can prevent the realization of the noblest social ideals of which the world has dreamed.

SHAILER MATHEWS: "THE EVOLUTION OF THE NEW SOCIETY"[2]

There is disappointment in store for the man who looks to Jesus for specific teachings as to reform. He was singularly unconcerned with those specific injunctions with which the system of Moses teems. There was no lack of vices within the Roman Empire, not yet feeling the weakly revivifying touch of poverty and philosophy, against which he might have thundered, to say nothing of those larger questions that might be expected to engage the attention of a developing society. Yet with none of these did he concern himself. The gospel was to be no new collection of moral precepts to be forced upon a world already surfeited with good advice, but a power that should make towards righteousness. The process of the new birth of the Jewish and heathen world was not to be that of a new subjection to law, be it never so inspired, but that of a growth that showed itself through such institutions as the process of evolution might show necessary. The symbol of the new society was not to be that of stones, graven though they might be by the hand of God, but the seed which, planted in the field, grows, one knows not how, and in proper season produces the blade, and the ear, and the full corn in the ear.

Thus the general nature of this progress is described by Jesus as an evolution, although it could not be expected that he would use the word.

It is to be the transformation of existing powers. This does not, however, commit Jesus to the belief that all that is necessary for the attainment of a perfect ideal of social life is simply the development of a godless sociability. As has already appeared, Jesus looked upon the religious capacity of men as just as truly normal and human as any other of the capacities of human life. Accordingly,

[2] Shailer Mathews, *op. cit.*, pp. 202-204.

when he trusted to humanity to develop into something like normal living, it was because he had recognized the religious forces resident in human nature which were capable themselves of great development and which possessed the power of transforming character. The world, or the existing social environment in which the new society found itself, was to be won over to the Christian conceptions of social relations by virtue of the fact that it contained within it material which might be regenerated through an apprehended God. Jesus was no Christ for animals, but for men. Because the world was evil did not argue that it was unsavable. If the leaven was to leaven the lump, it must have been because the lump was leavenable. Out from the seething mass of men and women so largely under the control of evil purposes and unbrotherly ideals, there was to be formed a body whose ideals were to be noble and fraternal. They were to be the same individuals, but transformed; no longer the enemies one of another, but brothers, each looking not alone to his own affairs, but also in the spirit of helpfulness to the affairs of another.

W. RAUSCHENBUSCH: JESUS THE BUILDER OF THE NEW SOCIETY[3]

Undoubtedly one of the leading figures of the "social gospel" movement in America was Walter Rauschenbusch, who became Professor of Church History in Rochester Theological Seminary. Although his work on Christianity and the Social Crisis *first appeared in 1907, his understanding of Jesus of Nazareth is so close to that of Shailer Matthews, that a brief section of it may appropriately be included here.*

Luke says that the boy Jesus "advanced in wisdom and stature, and in favor with God and men"; that is, he grew in his intellectual, physical, religious, and social capacities. It is contrary to faith in the real humanity of our Lord to believe that he ever stopped growing. The story of his temptation is an account of a forward leap in his spiritual insight when he faced the problems of his Messianic

[3] Walter Rauschenbusch, *Christianity and the Social Crisis* (New York: The Macmillan Company, 1907), pp. 65-68. Reprinted by permission of the estate of W. Rauschenbush.

task. When a growing and daring mind puts his hand to a great work, his experiences in that work are bound to enlarge and correct his conception of the purpose and methods of the work. It is wholly in harmony with any true conception of the life of Jesus to believe that his conception of the kingdom became vaster and truer as he worked for the kingdom, and that he moved away from the inherited conceptions along the lines which our study has suggested.

But after all this has been said, it still remained a social hope. The kingdom of God is still a collective conception, involving the whole social life of man. It is not a matter of saving human atoms, but of saving the social organism. It is not a matter of getting individuals to heaven, but of transforming the life on earth into the harmony of heaven. If he put his trust in spiritual forces for the founding of a righteous society, it only proved his sagacity as a society-builder. If he began his work with the smallest social nuclei, it proved his patience and skill. But Jesus never fell into the fundamental heresy of later theology; he never viewed the human individual apart from human society; he never forgot the gregarious nature of man. His first appeal was to his nation. When they flocked about him and followed him in the early Galilean days, it looked as if by the sheer power of his spirit he would swing the national soul around to obey him, and he was happy. There must have been at least a possibility of that in his mind, for he counted it as guilt that the people failed to yield to him. He did not merely go through the motions of summoning the nation to fealty, knowing all the while that such a thing lay outside of his real plan. No one will understand the life of Jesus truly unless he has asked himself the question, What would have happened if the people as a whole had accepted the spiritual leadership of Jesus? The rejection of his reign involved the political doom of the Galilean cities and of Jerusalem; would the acceptance of his reign have involved no political consequences? The tone of sadness in his later ministry was not due simply to the approach of his personal death, but to the consciousness that his purpose for his nation had failed. He began then to draw his disciples more closely about him and to create the nucleus of a new nation within the old; it was the best thing that remained for him to do, but he had hoped to do better. He also rose then to the conviction that he would return and accomplish in the future what he had hoped to accomplish during his earthly life. The hope of the Coming and the organization of the Church together enshrine the social element of Christianity; the one postpones it, the other partly realizes it. Both are the results of a faith that rose triumphant over death, and laid the foundations of a new commonwealth of God even before the old had been shaken to ruins.

All the teaching of Jesus and all his thinking centred about the hope of the kingdom of God. His moral teachings get their real meaning only when viewed from that centre. He was not a Greek philosopher or Hindu pundit teaching the individual the way of emancipation from the world and its passions, but a Hebrew prophet preparing men for the righteous social order. The goodness which he sought to create in men was always the goodness that would enable them to live rightly with their fellow-men and to constitute a true social life.

All human goodness must be social goodness. Man is fundamentally gregarious and his morality consists in being a good member of his community. A man is moral when he is social; he is immoral when he is anti-social. The highest type of goodness is that which puts freely at the service of the community all that a man is and can. The highest type of badness is that which uses up the wealth and happiness and virtue of the community to please self. All this ought to go without saying, but in fact religious ethics in the past has largely spent its force in detaching men from their community, from marriage and property, from interest in political and social tasks.

The fundamental virtue in the ethics of Jesus was love, because love is the society-making quality. Human life originates in love. It is love that holds together the basal human organization, the family. The physical expression of all love and friendship is the desire to get together and be together. Love creates fellowship. In the measure in which love increases in any social organism, it will hold together without coercion. If physical coercion is constantly necessary, it is proof that the social organization has not evoked the power of human affection and fraternity.

Hence when Jesus prepared men for the nobler social order of the kingdom of God, he tried to energize the faculty and habits of love and to stimulate the dormant faculty of devotion to the common good. Love with Jesus was not a flickering and wayward emotion, but the highest and most steadfast energy of a will bent on creating fellowship.

A. HARNACK: "GOD THE FATHER AND THE INFINITE VALUE OF THE HUMAN SOUL"[4]

Not in America, however, but in Germany the liberal view of Jesus as the teacher of an ethic of the Fatherhood of God and the Brotherhood of Men found its most classic expression. In the winter of 1899-1900 the renowned historian of the early Church and of Christian dogma, Adolph von Harnack, delivered a series of lectures at the University of Berlin under the title of "The Essence of Christianity." When these first came out in book form in 1900, they made an extraordinary impact, and were met with both "enthusiastic acclaim" and "bitter antagonism," as Rudolf Bultmann remarks in his Introduction to the 1957 Harper Torchbook edition of Harnack's work What Is Christianity?

Here with Harnack, if anywhere, the fundamental tendency of the liberal approach to Jesus becomes transparently clear. Jesus' proclamation, often in apocalyptic language, of the impending arrival of the kingdom of God is no real part of the "essence" of his message. Rather is it merely the outward and temporary shell, an accommodation to the local milieu *in which Jesus lived and thought. The true essential message of Jesus, which retains its meaning today and always, centers on God as Father and men as brothers.*

"The Gospel in the Gospel," says Harnack (p. 14), "is something so simple, something that speaks to us with so much power that it cannot easily be mistaken." He found that something simple in the clear and sympathetic eye with which Jesus looks out serenely upon man and the world and in the completely transparent language in which Jesus tells us that this our world is in the hands of the Father God in heaven (pp. 34-37).

Harnack appeared to believe that the only worthwhile reason for investigating the Gospels at all was that we might uncover something useful for us *in our own age (p. 13). So his aim in approaching them is to distinguish "what is permanent from what is fleeting, what is rudimentary from what is merely historical" (p. 14). With these words "merely historical" Har-*

[4] A. Harnack, *What Is Christianity?* (New York: Harper & Row, Publishers, 1957), pp. 63-74. All selections reprinted by permission of the publisher.

nack really lets the cat out of the bag. To shelve what is "merely historical" in the interest of something wrapped up in the history that is thought to be abiding truth is in fact to betray sound historical method. The function of the historian of Jesus' life is not forthwith to bring him or what is good in him into our own age, but to let him stand in the strange world of his own time, even if that means distancing Jesus from us and even if it is inconvenient for Christian theology and Christian ethics. Only so can we liberate ourselves from the peril of modernizing Jesus and so of misinterpreting him.

To our modern way of thinking and feeling, Christ's message appears in the clearest and most direct light when grasped in connexion with the idea of God the Father and the infinite value of the human soul.[5] Here the elements which I would describe as the restful and restgiving in Jesus' message, and which are comprehended in the idea of our being children of God, find expression. I call them *restful* in contrast with the impulsive and stirring elements; although it is just they that are informed with a special strength. But the fact that the whole of Jesus' message may be reduced to these two heads—God as the Father, and the human soul so ennobled that it can and does unite with him—shows us that the Gospel is in nowise a positive religion like the rest; that it contains no statutory or particularistic elements; *that it is, therefore, religion itself.* It is superior to all antithesis and tension between this world and a world to come, between reason and ecstasy, between work and isolation from the world, between Judaism and Hellenism. It can dominate them all, and there is no factor of earthly life to which it is confined or necessarily tied down. Let us, however, get a clearer idea of what being children of God, in Jesus' sense, means, by briefly considering four groups containing sayings of his, or, as the case may be, a single saying, viz.:—(1) The Lord's Prayer; (2) that utterance, "Rejoice not that the spirits are subject unto you; but rather rejoice because your names are written in heaven"; (3) the saying, "Are not two sparrows sold for a farthing? and one of

[5] Harnack maintained that the essentials of Jesus' teaching can be listed under three heads: the kingdom of God and its coming; God the Father and the infinite value of the human soul; the higher righteousness and the commandment of love (*What Is Christianity?* p. 51) [Ed.].

them shall not fall on the ground without your Father. But the very hairs of your head are all numbered"; (4) the utterance, "What shall it profit a man if he shall gain the whole world and lose his own soul?"

Let us take the Lord's Prayer first. It was communicated by Jesus to his disciples at a particularly solemn moment. They had asked him to teach them how to pray, as John the Baptist had taught his disciples. Thereupon he uttered the Lord's Prayer. It is by their prayers that the character of the higher religions is determined. But this prayer was spoken—as every one must feel who has ever given it a thought in his soul—by one who has overcome all inner unrest, or overcomes it the moment that he goes before God. The very apostrophe of the prayer, "Our Father," exhibits the steady faith of the man who knows that he is safe in God, and it tells us that he is certain of being heard. Not to hurl violent desires at heaven or to obtain this or that earthly blessing does he pray, but to preserve the power which he already possesses and strengthen the union with God in which he lives. No one, then, can utter this prayer unless his heart is in profound peace and his mind wholly concentrated on the inner relation of the soul with God. All other prayers are of a lower order, for they contain particularistic elements, or are so framed that in some way or other they stir the imagination in regard to the things of sense as well; whilst this prayer leads us away from everything to the height where the soul is alone with its God. And yet the earthly element is not absent. The whole of the second half of the prayer deals with earthly relations, but they are placed in the light of the Eternal. In vain will you look for any request for particular gifts of grace, or special blessings, even of a spiritual kind. "All else shall be added unto you." The name of God, His will, and His kingdom—these elements of rest and permanence are poured out over the earthly relations as well. Everything that is small and selfish melts away, and only four things are left with regard to which it is worth while to pray—the daily bread, the daily trespass, the daily temptations, and the evil in life. There is nothing in the Gospels that tells us more certainly what the Gospel is, and what sort of disposition and temper it produces, than the Lord's Prayer. With this prayer we ought also to confront all those who disparage the Gospel by representing it as an ascetic or ecstatic or sociological pronouncement. It shows the Gospel to be the Fatherhood of God applied to the whole of life; to be an inner union with God's will and God's kingdom, and a joyous certainty of the possession of eternal blessings and protection from evil.

As to the second utterance: when Jesus says "Rejoice not that the spirits are subject unto you, but rejoice rather that your names are written in heaven," it is another way of laying special emphasis on the idea that the all-important element in this religion is the consciousness of being safe in God. The greatest achievements, nay the very works which are done in the strength of this religion, fall below the assurance, at once humble and proud, of resting for time and eternity under the fatherly care of God. Moreover, the genuineness, nay the actual existence, of religious experience is to be measured, not by any transcendency of feeling nor by great deeds that all men can see, but by the joy and the peace which are diffused through the soul that can say "My Father."

How far did Christ carry this idea of the fatherly providence of God? Here we come to the third saying: "Are not two sparrows sold for a farthing? and one of them shall not fall to the ground without your Father. But the very hairs of your head are all numbered." The assurance that God rules is to go as far as our fears go, nay, as far as life itself—life down even to its smallest manifestations in the order of nature. It was to disabuse his disciples of the fear of evil and the terrors of death that he gave them the sayings about the sparrows and the flowers of the field; they are to learn how to see the hand of the living God everywhere in life, and in death too.

Finally, in asking—and after what has gone before the question will not sound surprising—"What shall it profit a man if he shall gain the whole world and lose his own soul?" he put a man's value as high as it can be put. The man who can say "My Father" to the Being who rules heaven and earth, is thereby raised above heaven and earth, and himself has a value which is higher than all the fabric of this world. But this great saying took the stern tone of a warning. He offered them a gift and with it set them a task. How different was the Greek doctrine! Plato, it is true, had already sung the great hymn of the mind; he had distinguished it from the whole world of appearance and maintained its eternal origin. But the mind which he meant was the knowing mind; he contrasted it with blind, insensible matter; his message made its appeal to the wise. Jesus Christ calls to every poor soul; he calls to every one who bears a human face: You are children of the living God, and not only better than many sparrows but of more value than the whole world.

The value of a truly great man, as I saw it put lately, consists in his increasing the value of all mankind. It is here, truly, that the highest significance of great men lies: to have enhanced, that is, to have progressively given effect to human value, to the value of that race of men which has risen up out of the dull ground of Nature. But Jesus Christ was the first to bring the value of every human soul to light, and what he did no one can any more undo. We may take up what relation to him we will: in the history of the past no one can refuse to recognise that it was he who raised humanity to this level.

This highest estimate of a man's value is based on a transvaluation of all values. To the man who boasts of his possessions he says: "Thou fool." He confronts everyone with the thought: "Whosoever will lose his life shall save it." He can even say: "He that hateth his life in this world shall keep it unto life eternal." This is the transvaluation of values of which many before him had a dim idea; of which they perceived the truth as through a veil; the redeeming power of which—that blessed mystery—they felt in advance. He was the first to give it calm, simple, and fearless expression, as though it were a truth which grew on every tree. It was just this that stamped his peculiar genius, that he gave perfectly simple expression to profound and all-important truths, as though they could not be otherwise; as though he were uttering something that was self-evident; as though he were only reminding men of what they all know already, because it lives in the innermost part of their souls.

In the combination of these ideas—God the Father, Providence, the position of men as God's children, the infinite value of the human soul—the whole Gospel is expressed. But we must recognise what a paradox it all is; nay, that the paradox of religion here for the first time finds its full expression. Measured by the experience of the senses and by exact knowledge, not only are the different religions a paradox, but so are all religious phenomena. They introduce an element, and pronounce it to be the most important of all, which is not cognisable by the senses and flies in the face of things as they are actually constituted. But all religions other than Christianity are in some way or other so bound up with the things of the world that they involve an element of earthly advantage, or, as the case may be, are akin in their substance to the intellectual and spiritual condition of a definite epoch. But what can be less obvious than the statement: the hairs of your head are all numbered; you have a supernatural value; you can put yourselves into the hands of a power which no one has seen? Either that is nonsense, or else it is the utmost development of which religion is capable; no longer a mere phenomenon accompanying the life of the senses, a co-efficient, a transfiguration of certain parts of that life, but something which sets up a paramount title to be the first and the only fact that reveals the fundamental basis and meaning of life. Religion subordinates to itself the whole motley world of phenomena, and defies that world if it claims to be the only real one. Religion gives us only a single experience, but one which presents the world in a new light: the Eternal appears; time becomes means to an end; man is seen to be on the side of the Eternal. This was certainly Jesus' meaning, and to take anything from it is to destroy it. In applying the idea of Providence to the whole of humanity and the world without any exception; in showing that humanity is rooted in the Eternal; in proclaiming the fact that we are God's children as at once a gift and a task, he took a firm grip of all fumbling and stammering attempts at religion and brought them to their issue. Once more let it be said: we may assume what position we will in regard to him and his message, certain it is that thence onward the value of our race is enhanced; human lives, nay, we ourselves, have become dearer to one another. A man may know it or not, but a real reverence for humanity follows from the practical recognition of God as the Father of us all. To represent the Gospel as an ethical message is no depreciation of its value. The ethical system which Jesus found prevailing in his nation was both ample and profound. To judge the moral ideas of the Pharisees solely by their childish and casuistical aspects is not fair. By being bound up with religious worship and petrified in ritual observance, the morality of holiness had, indeed, been transformed into something that was the clean opposite of it. But all was not yet hard and dead; there was some life still left in the deeper parts of the system. To those who questioned him Jesus could still answer: "You have the law, keep it; you know best yourselves what you have to do; the sum of the law is, as you yourselves say, to love God and your neighbour." Nevertheless, there is a sphere of ethical thought which is peculiarly expressive of Jesus' Gospel. Let us make this clear by citing four points.

Firstly: Jesus severed the connexion existing in his day between ethics and the external forms of religious worship and technical observance. He would have absolutely nothing to do with the purposeful and self-seeking pursuit of "good works" in combination with the ritual of worship. He exhibited an indignant contempt for those who allow their neighbours, nay, even their parents, to starve, and on the other hand send gifts to the temple. He will have no compromise in the matter. Love and mercy are ends in themselves; they lose all value and are put to shame by having to be anything else than the service of one's neighbour.

Secondly: in all questions of morality he goes straight to the root, that is, to the disposition and the intention. It is only thus that what he calls the "higher righteousness" can be understood. The "higher righteousness" is the righteousness that will stand when the depths of the heart are probed. Here, again, we have something that is seemingly very simple and self-evident. Yet the truth, as he uttered it, took the severe form: "It was said of old . . . but I say unto you." After all, then, the truth was something new; he was aware that it had never yet been expressed in such a consistent form and with such claims to supremacy. A large portion of the so-called Sermon on the Mount is occupied with what he says when he goes in detail through the several departments of human relationships and human failings so as to bring the disposition and intention to light in each case, to judge a man's works by them, and on them to hang heaven and hell.

Thirdly: what he freed from its connexion with self-seeking and ritual elements, and recognised as the moral principle, he reduces to *one* root and to *one* motive—love. He knows of no other, and love itself, whether it takes the form of love of one's neighbour or of one's enemy, or the love of the Samaritan, is of one kind only. It must completely fill the soul; it is what remains when the soul dies to itself. In this sense love is the new life already begun. But it is always the love which *serves,* and only in this function does it exist and live.

Fourthly: we saw that Jesus freed the moral element from all alien connexions, even from its alliance with the public religion. Therefore to say that the Gospel is a matter of ordinary morality is not to misunderstand him. And yet there is one all-important point where he combines religion and morality. It is a point which must be felt; it is not easy to define. In view of the Beatitudes it may, perhaps, best be described as *humility.* Jesus made love and humility one. Humility is not a virtue by itself; but it is pure receptivity, the expression of inner need, the prayer for God's grace and forgiveness, in a word, the opening up of the heart to God. In Jesus' view, this humility, which is the love of God of which we are capable—take, for instance, the parable of the Pharisee and the publican—is an abiding disposition towards the good, and that out of which everything that is good springs and grows. "Forgive us our trespasses even as we forgive them that trespass against us" is the prayer at once of humility and of love. This, then, is the source and origin of the love of one's neighbour; the poor in spirit and those who hunger and thirst after righteousness are also the peacemakers and the merciful.

It was in this sense that Jesus combined religion and morality, and in this sense religion may be called the soul of morality, and morality the body of religion. We can thus understand how it was that Jesus could place the love of God and the love of one's neighbour side by side; the love of one's neighbour is the only practical proof on earth of that love of God which is strong in humility.

In thus expressing his message of the higher righteousness and the new commandment of love in these four leading thoughts, Jesus defined the sphere of the ethical in a way in which no one before him had ever defined it. But should we be threatened with doubts as to what he meant, we must steep ourselves again and again in the Beatitudes of the Sermon on the Mount. They contain his ethics and his religion, united at the root, and freed from all external and particularistic elements.

A. HARNACK: "THE GOSPEL AND THE POOR, OR THE SOCIAL QUESTION" [5]

The bearings of the Gospel in regard to the social question form the second point which we proposed to consider. It is closely akin to the first. Here also we encounter different views prevalent at the present moment, or, to be more exact, two views, which are mutually opposed. We are told, on the one hand, that the Gospel was in the main a great social message to the poor, and that everything else in it is of secondary importance—mere contemporary wrapping, ancient tradition, or new forms supplied by the first generations of Christians. Jesus, they say, was a great social reformer, who aimed at relieving the lower classes from the wretched

[5] A. Harnack, *op. cit.*, pp. 88-92.

condition in which they were languishing; he set up a social programme which embraced the equality of all men, relief from economical distress, and deliverance from misery and oppression. It is only so, they add, that he can be understood, and therefore so he was; or perhaps—so he was, because it is only so that we can understand him. For years books and pamphlets have been written dealing with the Gospel in this sense; well-meant performances which aim at thus providing Jesus with a defence and a recommendation. But amongst those who take the Gospel to be an essentially social message there are also some who draw the opposite conclusion. By trying to prove that Jesus' message was wholly directed to bringing about an economical reform, they declare the Gospel to be an entirely Utopian and useless programme; the view, they say, which Jesus took of the world was gentle, but also weak; coming himself from the lower and oppressed classes, he shared the suspicion entertained by small people of the great and the rich; he abhorred all profitable trade and business; he failed to understand the necessity of acquiring wealth; and accordingly he shaped his programme so as to disseminate pauperism in the "world"—to him the world was Palestine—and then, by way of contrast with the misery on earth, to build up a kingdom in heaven; a programme unrealisable in itself, and offensive to men of energy. This, or something like this, is the view held by another section of those who identify the Gospel with a social message.

Opposed to this group of persons, united in the way in which they look at the Gospel but divided in their opinions in regard to it, there is another group upon whom it makes quite a different impression. They assert that as for any direct interest on Jesus' part in the economical and social conditions of his age; nay, further, as for any rudimentary interest in economical questions in general, it is only read into the Gospel, and that with economical questions the Gospel has absolutely nothing to do. Jesus, they say, certainly borrowed illustrations and examples from the domain of economics, and took a personal interest in the poor, the sick, and the miserable, but his purely religious teaching and his saving activity were in no way directed to any improvement in their earthly position: to say that his objects and intentions were of a social character is to secularize them. Nay, there are not a few among us who think him, like themselves, a "Conservative," who respected all these existing social differences and ordinances as "divinely ordained."

The voices which make themselves heard here are, as you will observe, very different, and the different points of view are defended with zeal and pertinacity. Now, if we are to try to find the position which corresponds to the facts, there is, first of all, a brief remark to be made on the age in which Jesus lived. Our knowledge of the social conditions in Palestine in his age and for some considerable time previously does not go very far; but there are certain leading features of it which we can establish, and two things more particularly which we can assert.

The governing classes, to which, above all, the Pharisees, and also the priests, belonged—the latter partly in alliance with the temporal rulers—had little feeling for the needs of the people. The condition of those classes may not have been much worse than it generally is at all times and in all nations, but it was bad. Moreover, there was here the additional circumstance that mercy and sympathy with the poor had been put into the background by devotion to public worship and to the cult of "righteousness." Oppression and tyranny on the part of the rich had long become a standing and inexhaustible theme with the Psalmists and with all men of any warm feelings. Jesus, too, could not have spoken of the rich as he did speak, unless they had grossly neglected their duties.

In the poor and oppressed classes, in the huge mass of want and evil, amongst the multitude of people for whom the word "misery" is often only another expression for the word "life," nay, is life itself—in this multitude there were groups of people at that time, as we can surely see, who, with fervent and steadfast hope, were hanging upon the promises and consoling words of their God, waiting in humility and patience for the day when their deliverance was to come. Often too poor to pay even for the barest advantages and privileges of public worship, oppressed, thrust aside, and unjustly treated, they could not raise their eyes to the temple; but they looked to the God of Israel, and fervent prayers went up to him: "Watchman, what of the night?" Thus their hearts were opened to God and ready to receive him, and in many of the Psalms, and in the later Jewish literature which was akin to them, the word "poor" directly denotes those who have their hearts open and are waiting for the consolation of Israel. Jesus found this usage of speech in existence and adopted it. Therefore when we come across the expression "the poor" in the Gospels we must not think, without further ceremony, of the poor in the economic sense. As a matter of fact, poverty in the economic sense coincided to a large extent in those days with religious humility and an openness of the heart towards God, in contrast with the elevated "practice of virtue" of the Pharisees and its routine observance in "righteousness." But if this were the prevailing condition of affairs, then it is clear that our modern categories of "poor" and "rich" cannot be unreservedly transferred to that age.

PART THREE

JESUS IN THE TWENTIETH CENTURY

7

Albert Schweitzer: The Wind of Change

Schweitzer's The Quest of the Historical Jesus *was first published in the early years of this century under its German title of* Von Reimarus zu Wrede. *It was subsequently to become a great landmark in Jesus research, although Schweitzer's own view of the life of Jesus is confined to the last two chapters and is to be found more fully developed in his other well known work,* The Mystery of the Kingdom of God, *trans. W. Lowrie (London, 1925).*

By far the largest part of The Quest *is given to an elaborate critique of the Liberal Lives of Jesus, a fact which hardly justifies the description once made of it as "a cemetery of departed hypotheses." As we noted in the Introduction, Schweitzer's quarrel with the authors of those Lives was that they saw Jesus through colored spectacles and depicted him according to their own ideals. But Schweitzer certainly did not abandon the idea that it was possible to take hold of Jesus as a strictly historical phenomenon. Only, in order to do so he followed Johannes Weiss in fastening on to the very feature of Jesus' history that the Liberals rejected as but the temporary integument of Jesus' true historical contribution to mankind. In other words he put Jesus' expectation of God's coming intervention in history at the very center and portrayed Jesus as one whose whole life was geared up to God's imminent cataclysmic overthrow of world history. Latterly he sent out his followers as bearers of this news, but when in fact the final crisis did not come, he surrendered himself to a martyr death in the hope that he might accomplish it.*

Schweitzer's picture of Jesus arose of course from his own critical understanding of the Gospels, especially of Mark and Matthew. The Liberals had taken recourse to Mark as the basic document for their biographies of Jesus, and from the standpoint of modern psychology had read Mark as a record of the progressive development of Jesus' psychological consciousness. Schweitzer considered on the contrary that Mark offered a quite inadequate basis for comprehending the historical Jesus and that Mark's record was inherently unintelligible. The only way to make sense of Jesus' history was to take full account of the tenth and eleventh chapters of Matthew, and in particular of the crucial verse Matthew 10:23: "When they persecute you in one city, flee to another. Verily I say to you that you will not have gone through all the cities of Israel before the Son of Man comes." This prediction of the coming of the Son of Man in the very near future or rather the nonfulfilment of the prediction provided for Schweitzer the real clue to Jesus' life, and revealed the true direction of that life. The eschatological discourses of Matthew 10 and 11 make it clear that Jesus did anticipate the immediate coming of the last things and did believe that he would soon be transformed into a new condition at the dawning of the supernatural world. The sufferings Jesus saw at hand were the apocalyptic woes preceding the last days, not his passion and death as the Liberals assumed from the prophecies of suffering in Mark (see Schweitzer, The Quest, *pp. 358-362).*

When the disciples returned from their tour of the cities of Israel and still the new world had not arrived, Jesus was at last constrained to force the hand of God as it were—so overwhelmed was he with the idea that the end of the days was very close. The following words from Schweitzer show how he thought that Jesus purposely gave himself to setting the eschatological process in motion.[1]

The Baptist and Jesus are not borne upon the current of a general eschatological movement. The period offers no events calculated to give an impulse to eschatological enthusiasm. They themselves set the times in motion by acting, by creating

[1] A. Schweitzer, *The Quest of the Historical Jesus,* trans. W. Montgomery (London: A. and C. Black, 1922), pp. 368-369.

eschatological facts. It is this mighty creative force which constitutes the difficulty in grasping historically the eschatology of Jesus and the Baptist. Instead of literary artifice speaking out of a distant imaginary past, there now enter into the field of eschatology men, living, acting men. It was the only time when that ever happened in Jewish eschatology.

There is silence all around. The Baptist appears, and cries: "Repent, for the Kingdom of Heaven is at hand." Soon after that comes Jesus, and in the knowledge that He is the coming Son of Man lays hold of the wheel of the world to set it moving on that last revolution which is to bring all ordinary history to a close. It refuses to turn and He throws Himself upon it. Then it does turn; and crushes Him. Instead of bringing in the eschatological conditions, He has destroyed them. The wheel rolls onward, and the mangled body of the one immeasurably great Man, who was strong enough to think of Himself as the spiritual ruler of mankind and to bend history to His purpose is hanging upon it still. That is His victory and His reign."

Schweitzer stood the normal Liberal position on Jesus on its head. The Liberals regarded Jesus' apocalyptic dogma merely as the outer shell enclosing and concealing his true historical being, a temporary accommodation to his time and place. Schweitzer found in the "apocalyptic dogmatic" element the key to the real history of Jesus.

Since Schweitzer the best New Testament scholarship has inevitably had to reckon with Jesus' eschatology as a central and decisive factor in his historical appearance. Brilliant as Schweitzer's contribution was, however, not many have agreed entirely with his thoroughgoing eschatological portrait of Jesus. His interpretation of Matthew 10 and 11 and particularly of Matthew 10:23 has been called seriously into question. Even if Jesus seems to have expected the End of all things soon (and we distort the evidence of the Gospels if we neglect or interpret away the references to the future in his message of the kingdom of God), it is open to debate whether the actual time factor *as such was so very important to Jesus as Schweitzer suggested. Then again the problem of Jesus' use of the Son of Man designation in its many details has been widely canvassed in the past half century, and certainly not everyone would agree that Jesus thought of himself as the coming Son of Man in Schweitzer's sense. There is the view, among many other views on the Son of Man put forward in recent years, that Jesus did predict the coming of the Son of Man, but he was speaking not of himself but of another eschatological figure. There is also the view that Jesus did not want to indulge in apocalyptic elaboration about the future kingdom at all or to impart teaching about the future Son of Man, but simply brought in the coming Son of Man to confirm the decisiveness of his own offer of salvation in the present. Enough has been said to show that there are viable alternative interpretations of a saying like Matthew 10:23 to that of Schweitzer.*

Views on Jesus in our time have tended to oscillate between Harnack's picture of the uniquely great ethical teacher and Schweitzer's picture of the fervent apocalypticist, whose ethic can only be described as an Interimsethik, *applicable only to the short interval between Jesus' death and God's impending irruption into history. What was the secret of Jesus' illumination? Did his ethic derive its edge and urgency from his own profound inward awareness of the will of God and was his expectation and proclamation of the imminent End of things secondary to that? Or was it in fact his acute sense of the impending closure of world history that gave to his moral teaching its immediacy and authority? The relation of Jesus' ethics and his eschatology has certainly been a burning question. Perhaps we do not have the means for a final solution because the Gospels do not disclose what went on in the mind of Jesus.*

One of the supreme merits of Schweitzer's understanding of Jesus is that he sets Jesus foursquare in the true historical framework of his own day, in the first-century world of Jewish apocalyptic so remote and alien from us. Schweitzer's Jesus consequently is neither congenial nor winsome nor attractive nor any of the nice things many of us like to call him. But there is health and freedom and one suspects truth in this kind of distancing of Jesus from us, for it saves us from sentimentalizing him by making him into our own sort of contemporary "good man." This distant Jesus can come to us now, as Schweitzer thinks, not as an easily understood "modern," but only as "One unknown."

It was no small matter, therefore, that in the course of the critical study of the Life of Jesus, after a resistance lasting for two generations, during which first one expedient was tried and then another, theology was forced by genuine history to begin to doubt the artificial history with which it had thought to give new life to our Christianity, and to yield to the facts, which, as Wrede strikingly said, are sometimes the most radical critics of all. History will force it to find a way to transcend history, and to fight for the lordship and rule of Jesus over this world with weapons tempered in a different forge.

We are experiencing what Paul experienced. In the very moment when we were coming nearer to the historical Jesus than men had ever come before, and were already stretching out our hands to draw Him into our own time, we have been obliged to give up the attempt and acknowledge our failure in that paradoxical saying: "If we have known Christ after the flesh yet henceforth know we Him no more." And further we must be prepared to find that the historical knowledge of the personality and life of Jesus will not be a help, but perhaps even an offence to religion.

But the truth is, it is not Jesus as historically known, but Jesus as spiritually arisen within men, who is significant for our time and can help it. Not the historical Jesus, but the spirit which goes forth from Him and in the spirits of men strives for new influence and rule, is that which overcomes the world.

It is not given to history to disengage that which is abiding and eternal in the being of Jesus from the historical forms in which it worked itself out, and to introduce it into our world as a living influence. It has toiled in vain at this undertaking. As a water-plant is beautiful so long as it is growing in the water, but once torn from its roots, withers and becomes unrecognisable, so it is with the historical Jesus when He is wrenched loose from the soil of eschatology, and the attempt is made to conceive Him "historically" as a Being not subject to temporal conditions. The abiding and eternal in Jesus is absolutely independent of historical knowledge and can only be understood by contact with His spirit which is still at work in the world. In proportion as we have the Spirit of Jesus we have the true knowledge of Jesus.

Jesus as a concrete historical personality remains a stranger to our time, but His spirit, which lies hidden in His words, is known in simplicity, and its influence is direct. Every saying contains in its own way the whole Jesus. The very strangeness and unconditionedness in which He stands before us makes it easier for individuals to find their own personal standpoint in regard to Him.

Men feared that to admit the claims of eschatology would abolish the significance of His words for our time; and hence there was a feverish eagerness to discover in them any elements that might be considered not eschatologically conditioned. When any sayings were found of which the wording did not absolutely imply an eschatological connexion there was great jubilation—these at least had been saved uninjured from the coming *débâcle.*

But in reality that which is eternal in the words of Jesus is due to the very fact that they are based on an eschatological world-view, and contain the expression of a mind for which the contemporary world with its historical and social circumstances no longer had any existence. They are appropriate, therefore, to any world, for in every world they raise the man who dares to meet their challenge, and does not turn and twist them into meaninglessness, above his world and his time, making him inwardly free, so that he is fitted to be, in his own world and in his own time, a simple channel of the power of Jesus.

Modern Lives of Jesus are too general in their scope. They aim at influencing, by giving a complete impression of the life of Jesus, a whole community. But the historical Jesus, as He is depicted in the Gospels, influenced individuals by the individual word. They understood Him so far as it was necessary for them to understand, without forming any conception of His life as a whole, since this in its ultimate aims remained a mystery even for the disciples.

Because it is thus preoccupied with the general, the universal, modern theology is determined to find its world-accepting ethic in the teaching of Jesus. Therein lies its weakness. The world affirms itself automatically; the modern spirit cannot but affirm it. But why on that account abolish the conflict between modern life, with the world-affirming spirit which inspires it as a whole, and the world-negating spirit of Jesus? Why spare the spirit of the individual man its appointed task of fighting its way through the world-negation of Jesus, of contending with Him at every step over the value of material and intellectual goods—a conflict in which it may never rest? For the general, for the institutions of society, the rule is: affirmation of the world, in conscious opposition to the view of Jesus, on the ground that the world has affirmed itself! This general affirmation of the world, however, if it is to be Christian, must in the individual spirit be Christianised and transfigured by the personal rejection of the world which is preached in the sayings of Jesus. It is only by means of the tension thus set up that religious energy can be communicated to our time. There was a danger that modern theology, for the sake of peace, would deny the world-negation in the sayings of Jesus, with which Protestantism was out of sympathy, and thus unstring the bow and make Protestantism a mere sociological instead of a religious force. There was perhaps also a danger of inward insincerity, in the fact that it refused to admit to itself and others that it maintained its affirmation of the world in opposition to the sayings of Jesus, simply because it could not do otherwise.

For that reason it is a good thing that the true historical Jesus should overthrow the modern Jesus, should rise up against the modern spirit and send upon earth, not peace, but a sword. He was not teacher, not a casuist; He was an imperious ruler. It was because He was so in His inmost being that He could think of Himself as the Son of Man. That was only the temporally conditioned expression of the fact that He was an authoritative ruler. The names in which men expressed their recognition of Him as such, Messiah, Son of Man, Son of God, have become for us historical parables. We can find no designation which expresses what He is for us.

He comes to us as One unknown, without a name, as of old, by the lakeside, He came to those men who knew Him not. He speaks to us the same word: "Follow thou me!" and sets us to the tasks which He has to fulfil for our time. He commands. And to those who obey Him, whether they be wise or simple, He will reveal Himself in the toils, the conflicts, the sufferings which they shall pass through in His fellowship, and, as an ineffable mystery, they shall learn in their own experience Who He is.[2]

[2] A. Schweitzer, *The Quest of the Historical Jesus,* trans. W. Montgomery (London: A. and C. Black, 1922), pp. 397-401. Reprinted by permission of the publisher.

8

The Resilience of Liberal Views of Jesus

Other voices as well as Schweitzer's were raised in protest at the Liberals' representations of Jesus. New methods of Gospel criticism that came to full fruition in the years just after the First World War were threatening to shatter the earlier confidence that the Gospels and especially Mark could be accepted as reliable accounts of the development of Jesus' life or personality in any biographical sense.

Despite all this, typically liberal approaches to Jesus have survived throughout the present century until now. Outstanding examples are T. R. Glover's The Jesus of History *(1917) in England and S. J. Case's* Jesus—a New Biography *(1927) in America.*

Glover deals at some length with the "liberal" themes of the "domestic life of Jesus," his "words and looks," "playfulness of speech," "movements of feeling," "habits of thought" —Jesus' great mission in life was to encourage all men eventually to rethink the idea of God. And the question arises: are not these modern concerns? Are the Gospel texts really interested in these matters?

Case had undoubtedly appropriated the newer insights of Gospel criticism; he makes much of the fact that the Gospels were the products of the social and communal life of the early Church, and that the ascription to Jesus of miraculous powers and supernatural attributes reflected the Church's belief. Moreover, although Case is very much alive to the apocalyptic-eschatological element in Jesus' message, he sees it as incidental to Jesus' real historical intention, which is his dominating ambition "to impel his hearers to higher attainments in righteousness." Jesus is in fact a prophet of moral reform.

T. R. GLOVER: THE KINGDOM AS THE UNION OF THE INDIVIDUAL SOUL WITH GOD [1]

We have to remark how firmly Jesus believes in his Gospel of God and man needing each other and finding each other—his "good news," as he calls it. He bases all on his faith in what has been called "Man's incurable religious instinct"—that instinct in the human heart that must have God—and in God's response to that instinct which He Himself implanted, and which is no accident found here and missing there, but a genuine God-given characteristic of every man, whatever his temperament or his range in emotions may be, his swiftness or slowness of mind. The repeated parables of seed and leaven—the parables of vitality—again and again suggest his faith in his message, his conviction that God must have man and man must have God—that, as St. Augustine puts it, "Thou hast made us for Thyself, and our heart knows no rest till it rests in Thee" (*Conf.*, i. I). That is the essence of the Gospel.

How this union of the soul with God comes about, Jesus does not directly say, but there are many hints in his teaching that bear upon it. "The Kingdom of Heaven cometh not with observation," he said (Luke xvii. 20). Religious truth is not reached by "quick turns of self-applauding intellect," nor by demonstrations. It comes another way. The quiet familiarity with the deep true things of life, till on a sudden they are transfigured in the light of God, and truth is a new and glowing thing, independent of arguments and the strange evidence of thaumaturgy—this is the normal way; and Jesus holds by it. The great people, men of law and learning, want more; they want something to substantiate God's messages from without. If Jesus comes to them with a word from God, can he not prove its authenticity preferably with "a sign from the sky" (Mark viii. II)? For the signs he gives, and the evidence he suggests, are unsatisfactory. "And he sighed deeply in his spirit, and saith, 'Why doth this generation seek after a sign? Verily I say unto you, there shall no sign be given unto this generation.' So he left them and went up into the ship again and went away." That scene is drawn from life.

[1] T. R. Glover, *The Jesus of History* (London: S. C. M. Press, 1922), pp. 101-102. Reprinted by permission of the publisher.

S. J. CASE: "THE RELIGION JESUS LIVED"[2]

The prophet lived in a relation to God that was essentially a mystical experience. But it was not the type of mysticism that evaporated in an orgy of emotions. There was a wealth of feeling in the prophetic experience, but it was of the sort that gave to life a mighty ethical and spiritual drive. Jesus did not lose himself in God, as though the emotion were an end in itself. On the contrary, the divine seizure was for the sake of increasing righteousness in the world and contributing to human welfare. Its end was to be the establishment of the Kingdom. Yet Jesus was no maker of programs, no framer of agenda to be acted on by individuals or assemblies through all time to come. Nor was he a creator of moral or religious credenda once for all delivered to his followers. His religion struck its roots more deeply into the life of the soul—a soul that enjoyed perpetual communion with God its Father. Opinions and deeds, to be of value, must be the expressions of a pure heart. Make the tree itself good and the fruits thereof would be of proper quality.

For Jesus, who felt himself wholly in the grip of the Almighty, religion was essentially an experiential affair rooted in the spiritual impulses of the inner life. Deeds were performed and words were spoken out of the abundance of the heart. He who urged others to scrutinize their motives and sanctify their aspirations, was himself a living example of the individual whose piety springs forth spontaneously from the depths of his being.

[2] Shirley Jackson Case, *Jesus, A New Biography* (Chicago: The University of Chicago Press, 1927), pp. 386-387. Reprinted by permission of the publisher.

9

Popular Portraits of Jesus

T. R. Glover and S. J. Case, from whose works we have just quoted, were both professional biblical scholars. But in this century also there has been no end to the making of books on Jesus by writers who are neither professional theologians nor biblical critics. These popular delineations of Jesus have nearly all one feature in common—they clothe Jesus in modern garb, and the garb to be sure is that familiarly worn by the author himself. Out of the multitude of such presentations we select here only two.

The Life of Jesus *by J. Middleton Murry shows Jesus as the ideal man of the future. Murry has trenchant words of criticism for the Higher Critics of the Bible: "They have taken away my Master, and I know not where they have laid him"; criticism also for the rationalists for making Jesus altogether too human and for the orthodox theologians for not allowing him to be human. Murry was himself a literary critic of repute.*

The Divine Propagandist *by Lord Beaverbrook sets Jesus forth as the greatest of all propaganda experts. Beaverbrook was in fact a statesman and newspaper magnate, engrossed day by day with the mass media of communication and not a little skilled himself in handling the weapons of propaganda.*

Let the reader come straight from a perusal of the Gospels and ask whether the "ideal man of genius" and "propagandist" are not modern categories into which in each case, by an a priori *decision, the Jesus of history has been fitted.*

J. MIDDLETON MURRY: "THE MAN OF THE FUTURE" [1]

From Cæsarea Philippi, where the great decision was taken by himself and confirmed by God, Jesus went straight to his journey's end—Jerusalem and death. He had a choice of roads before him:

[1] J. Middleton Murry, *The Life of Jesus* (London: Jonathan Cape, 1926), pp. 207-211. Reprinted by permission of the publisher.

either to take the road east of Jordan through Decapolis and Herod's tetrarchy of Peræa; or to take the road west of Jordan, through Galilee and Samaria. Both were dangerous: on either hand he must pass through Herod's territory.

For himself, and a few inner disciples, he chose the latter; and it seems that others with the bulk of his Galilean followers—perhaps a few hundreds—took the common pilgrim road through Peræa to meet him again at the Jordan ford not far from Jericho.

He passed through Galilee concealed; yet he could not resist the desire to revisit for the last time his second home, 'the house' at Capernaum. On the road thither he told his disciples once more of his coming suffering—that he must be betrayed to death. 'But they could not understand,' says Mark, 'and they were afraid to ask him.'

'So they came to Capernaum,' Mark continues. 'And when he was in the house, he asked them: "What were you disputing about on the road?" '

There are no more pregnant words, in any history, than these bare and naïve sentences of Mark. Jesus did not know what his disciples had been disputing: he had been walking, silent and alone, on the road ahead of them: only the murmur of their petulant voices had reached him. They were afraid to speak to him; now he was become a being apart, whom they could no longer approach as in the old days. They could not understand his words: he had told them that he was to be betrayed.

That was new. Not that they did not understand it because it was new; they understood nothing of him now. But now for the first time Jesus spoke of his betrayal.

Was it a new thought that came to him as he strode ahead? Had he chosen betrayal, and his betrayer? The more one reads the gospel narrative, the more certain it seems that Jesus' betrayal and the manner and the agent of it were predetermined by himself.

Jesus had deliberately chosen the way of suffering and death; it was forced upon him by his consciousness of what he was. There was no place for the solitary son of God upon this earth, nor for a living Messiah in the world. Having chosen his ineluctable destiny, he made his face rigid to go to Jerusalem. He had chosen to die in Jerusalem, and to die at the feast of the Passover. He would be the sacrificial lamb of his people and of the world: 'as the sheep before the shearers is dumb, so he would open not his mouth.'

It was an unparalleled imagination. Two thousand years of history, through which its appeal to the soul of Western men has never been diminished, vindicate it as man's supreme achievement. That through the centuries it has been understood in a way a modern mind can no longer understand it as the self-sacrifice of God himself incarnate is of little moment: formulations change, but the spiritual verity is the same. What the devout Christian has worshipped in the God-man, we can revere in the man-God. He could not believe that a man was capable of so supreme an imagination; we can. That is the only difference. We understand the old forms: the spiritual verity shines through them for any man to see. But we know—simply because we belong to the twentieth century and must not reject our birthright—that the old forms are *forms*. We see their beauty and their necessity. The man who sees nothing in the great Christian dogmas but illusion and error, is blind indeed.

The Christian verity is a statement of this sublime imagination and act of the man Jesus. Two thousand years ago it appeared to those who contemplated it so sublime that it must be the imagination and the act of God. So, in the final contemplation, it was. In Jesus God was manifest as he has never since been manifest in man: but manifest in him, because he was wholly man. God is not manifest otherwise; he does not exist save in all the particularity of creation. Jesus was the supreme manifestation of God simply because he was the supreme manifestation of Man.

Faith in the God-man, knowledge of the man-God—both spring alike from contemplation of the imagination and act of the man Jesus. One is the response of a soul which says: No *man* could have conceived or done this thing; the other the response of the soul which says: No one but a man could have conceived or done it. Both are true. But the former truth belongs to the past; the latter to the future.

Yet see how close they come. For the believer in the God-man, the passion and the manner of Jesus was predetermined by God; for the believer in the man-God it was predetermined by himself. But for both alike *predetermined.* That is the essential. On this essential predetermination of his passion all rationalist lives of Jesus are wrecked. It is for the rationalist an element imported into the story by after-generations to correspond with their belief in his Godhead: for the rationalist and the liberal, Jesus is, however kindly they may put it, only the fanatic who lost his life at the head of a heretical and revolutionary movement. He did not, because he could not, predetermine the manner and day of his death. He could not do this because he was only a man. And for the rationalist and the liberal 'only a man' means 'only a man like me.' What they could not do, he could not do. Never was there yet a liberal or a rationalist life of Jesus that did not end on a note of sympathetic condescension: he did this, and it was very beautiful, but we understand better.

We do not understand better. To look for a liberal Jesus is mistaken. But it is mistaken, also, to do as the eschatologist and put him into an abyss of darkness, with the assurance that we cannot understand him. Understanding is not the faculty by which Jesus can be known: but intuition. We have to seize in act a greater spirit than our own, we have to pluck from the future, the man of the future. Jesus can be reached, if he can be reached at all, through the man of genius alone. But he will never be *understood.*

Jesus was not a fanatic who lost his life in a heretical movement. He was a new kind of man, who was inexorably driven by reason of his new faculties to believe himself the only son of God, and to seek the only death that was fitting for such a one. The manner of that death he predetermined for his own great ends. He was able to predetermine it because he was a man of new faculties and new powers.

To die at Jerusalem, as the Paschal Lamb, was not an easy thing to accomplish. At Jerusalem was a Roman procurator and a Roman garrison, ready indeed to do Roman justice upon him were he to appear as an enemy of the civil power. But what had he to do with the civil power? He was deliberately indifferent to it. And as for placing himself in a position in which he should die as a common criminal nothing could be more alien from his purpose. His purpose was to die as the suffering Messiah.

LORD BEAVERBROOK: "THE DIVINE PROPAGANDIST" [2]

Jesus now stands before us simply and nakedly as the greatest propagandist the world has ever known. In three years only he has to make an imprint on the human conscience which will last to eternity. In the pursuit of this object all minor considerations must be swept aside. Nothing matters except the preaching and practising

[2] Lord Beaverbrook, *The Divine Propagandist* (London, Melbourne, and Toronto: Heinemann, 1962), pp. 35-39. Reprinted by permission of The First Beaverbrook Foundation.

of the word. And the work requires extraordinary judgment and efficiency.

With all power in His hands Jesus has to choose the exact weapons and exert the right amount of influence to secure His purpose. There is the danger of converting the world not by a gradual and natural process of belief but by a revolutionary series of miracles. Conversely there is the risk that the seed may not germinate at all if the ground is too stony with disbelief.

The main propagandist weapons used are personality, example and oratory. His message was a personal one conveyed in the spoken word. So far as we know not one of His sayings was written down and circulated in His lifetime. His method therefore was different in many respects from that of the modern propagandist who has before him a large choice of instruments which are afforded to him.

All propaganda which is powerful and effective must be cumulative in character. It must increase in intensity as it proceeds, until ultimately it reaches a tone not far removed from violence. Thus, the campaign which begins with the Sermon on the Mount ends with the expulsion of the moneychangers from the Temple under the threat of mob-riot.

However laudable the aim, there was nothing of the "Gentle Jesus" in the propagandist who purified a church by overturning tables and driving the traffickers out with a whip. On the contrary His method was that of a ruthless efficiency.

But it is in dealing with the Pharisees, the Sadducees, the priests and the lawyers that Jesus is seen at His sternest. It was the essential aim of His propaganda to break down a system of religious formalism which obscured the plain word of God and overlaid the living soul of man with a series of minute observances. The Kingdom of God could not flourish in an atmosphere of long formal prayers and tithe collections.

The Gospels therefore are full of denunciations of existing religious authorities. Jesus disregards even His practice of social cheerfulness and the obligations of a guest when the Pharisee who entertains Him marvels that He does not wash His hands formally before eating. He answers with a tremendous denunciation: "Now do ye Pharisees make clean the outside of the cup and the platter; but your inward part is full of ravening and wickedness."

After the Pharisees, the lawyers. "Woe unto you, lawyers! for ye have taken away the key of knowledge: ye entered not in yourselves, and them that were entering in ye hindered."

And in another place may be found words addressed to the same class as violent as were ever addressed to any set of men: "Ye serpents, ye generation of vipers, how can ye escape the damnation of hell?"

So did Jesus, the relentless propagandist, fight the opponents of the Kingdom of God. It is probable that in denouncing the simony, the hypocrisy, the organised religiosity, the love of pomp and power, which defaced the contemporary Hebrew Church, He had a prophetic vision of what His own faith would suffer at the hands of the future formalists of the Christian Church.

Jesus, as a propagandist, is like a man desperately forewarning the disciples, who must try and tread in His footsteps age after age. A religion organised into a community, a creed, and a vested interest is in permanent danger of becoming an absolute impediment to the entry into the Kingdom of God.

Jesus is obviously more afraid of the Church as a potential enemy than He is of money or the world—because He is more bitter against the Churchmen.

10

Jesus Through Jewish Eyes

Some Jewish views on Jesus, mainly polemical, from the early centuries of our era, are embodied in the Jewish Talmud. They do not amount to much—Jesus' miracles are characterized as the acts of an accomplished sorcerer; he is said to have been an illegitimate child. If later centuries reveal a much more jaundiced attitude toward Jesus, we should not forget the hatred occasioned by long years of bitterness and persecution. Come the Middle Ages and the rise of the ghettoes, profoundly prejudiced Jewish histories of Jesus began to circulate widely. The best known of these histories is the Toledoth Yeshu. *For hundreds of years it enjoyed great popularity among the Jews—its avowed aim to discredit the reputed founder of Christianity.*

Fortunately bitterness and bias have not prevailed all the way. In more modern times, and particularly in our own century, a succession of Jewish scholars have ventured to investigate more constructively the significance of Jesus' life and teaching. Liberal Jewish estimates of Jesus, as one might expect, have been more positive and laudatory than orthodox Jewish.

GERALD FRIEDLÄNDER: SOME ORTHODOX JEWISH OBSERVATIONS ON JESUS [1]

Probably 1900 years ago, a teacher and a claimant to the Messiahship named Jesus, the son of Joseph and Mary, lived in Galilee. His apocalyptic dreams and his eschatological discourses induced his followers to recognize his Messianic claims, and this led to a conflict with the ruling authorities, i.e. the Roman Procurator. The death of Jesus did not destroy the movement he had set on foot.

[1] Gerald Friedländer, *The Jewish Sources of the Sermon on the Mount* (London: Routledge & Kegan Paul, 1910), pp. xviii f., 3, 9, 23, 58, 188-190, 262f. Reprinted by permission of the publisher.

His followers awaited his Parousia,[2] and meanwhile they remained within the camp of Pharisaic Judaism. This state continued until the destruction of Jerusalem in 70 C.E. In the early years of the second century the Gospels were written and Christianity arose as a new religion. . . .

Not only is the baptism story [Mark 1:9-11. Ed.] apocalyptic, but . . . practically all the genuine teaching of Jesus is apocalyptic. . . .

Much of his teaching could justly be called prophetic, but then, in all such cases, . . . he is merely repeating the identical words or re-enforcing the messages of the prophets of old. . . .

The Beatitudes have undoubtedly a lofty tone, but let us not forget that all that they teach can be found in Isaiah and the Psalms. Israel finds nothing new here. . . .

Jesus tried to abolish divorce [Mark 10:2-9. Ed.] but he failed. . . . Judaism again has nothing to learn from the negative teaching of Jesus. . . .

Jesus' absolute faith in Providence, unaccompanied by *any* effort on man's part, is not Jewish doctrine. . . . Trust in God is essential, but this does not mean a careless life. Man cannot, in spite of Jesus' teaching, live his life like the flowers and birds. . . .

All the teaching in the Sermon on the Mount, which is in harmony with the spirit of Judaism, is a possible charter for a world religion which is content to reckon Jesus of Nazareth as one of the many teachers of humanity—less inspired than the prophets of the Old Testament—whose vision was that of an apocalyptic dreamer, whose message was eschatological and therefore of little practical value for everyday life.

C. G. MONTEFIORE: JESUS AND THE RABBIS[3]

Montefiore, one-time president of the Liberal Jewish Synagogue, put Christian scholarship on the Gospels largely in his

[2] *Parousia* is a Greek term, used in the New Testament of the expected return of Christ in the End time [Ed.].

[3] C. G. Montefiore, *Some Elements of the Religions Teaching of Jesus According to the Synoptic Gospels* (London: Macmillan and Co., 1910), pp. 57-58, 112-113. Reprinted by permission of the publisher.

debt by his magnificent commentary on the Synoptic Gospels. All his writing on Jesus is remarkably open and fair-minded, not least the one we cite from here. At crucial points his judgments come surprisingly close to those of such recent Christian writers, for example, as G. Bornkamm.

The Rabbis attached no less value to repentance than Jesus. They sang its praises and its efficacy in a thousand tones. They, too, urged that God cared more for the repentant than for the just who had never yielded to sin. They, too, welcomed the sinner in his repentance. But to *seek out* the sinner, and, instead of avoiding the bad companion, to choose him as your friend in order to work his moral redemption, this was, I fancy, something new in the religious history of Israel. The methods which Jesus sometimes adopted for the cure of sin were original and startling. It does not follow that in a lesser man these methods would be either justified or successful. It is not every one who can imitate Jesus, and without harm to himself and with benefit to his companions become the friend of sinners.

Jesus seems (upon the slender evidence we have) to have perceived the good lurking under the evil. He could quench the evil and quicken the good by giving to the sinner somebody to admire and to love. He asked for service, and put it in the place of sin. The hatefulness of his past life was brought vividly to the mind of the sinner as the antithesis of his new affection and of his loving gratitude. It was, doubtless, often a daring method; even with Jesus it may not always have been successful. But it inaugurated a new idea: the idea of redemption, the idea of giving a fresh object of love and interest to the sinner, and so freeing him from his sin. The rescue and deliverance of the sinner through pity and love and personal service—the work and the method seem both alike due to the teacher of Nazareth. . . .

Even when we have to deal with so famous and characteristic an element of the teaching as the love of enemies, we must be careful to hold the scales with judicial impartiality. Jewish critics usually take the line that in the command, "Love your enemies," there is indeed an original feature, but that the feature, though it sounds well, is impracticable and therefore undesirable or harmful. Jewish ethics, they will tell you, say, "*Help,* and do good to, your enemy whenever occasion offers." This can be done, and therefore is done. Christian ethics say, "*Love* your enemy." This cannot be done, and is therefore always neglected, as, for instance, the history of the Jews for eighteen hundred years has so conspicuously proved.

It would take a long while to go into this criticism fully and fairly, as regards what it asserts both of Jewish teaching on the one hand, and of Christian teaching upon the other. We should have also to estimate the value of the Greek verb which we translate "love" in this particular connection, and decide how far there is a precise equivalence between the two. For all this there is no time. It would perhaps be found that the teaching of Jesus is here too on the lines of a few highest Rabbinic utterances, but that it goes beyond them in a sort of intense inwardness, in emotional fervour, and in the eager passion of genius. Here too the stress would perhaps have to be laid, to some extent at least, upon the way in which the teaching is expressed, as well as upon its actual subject-matter.

JOSEPH KLAUSNER: THE TRULY JEWISH JESUS? [4]

Klausner was born in Russia in 1874. Having become associated with the Zionist movement, he eventually studied in Heidelberg, and settled in Palestine in 1920, where he gained a notable reputation as writer and public worker. His book, Jesus of Nazareth, *is probably the fullest treatment of the subject from the Jewish side.*

The bias against the Pharisees in some of Jesus' sayings in the Gospels reflects, according to Klausner, the breach between the early Church and the Synagogue, and is no part of the teaching of the historical Jesus. Jesus Klausner claims wholly for Judaism. His ethical teaching, his main strength, has in its every item prototypes in the Jewish literature. He is "the most Jewish of Jews," and yet, as Klausner believes, he so exaggerates and extends the true Judaism that it becomes in the end non-Judaism.

There is no page in this volume, no step in the life-story of Jesus, and no line in his teaching on which is not stamped the seal

[4] Joseph Klausner, *Jesus of Nazareth,* trans. from the Hebrew edition of 1922 by H. Danby (London: George Allen & Unwin, 1948), pp. 413-414. Reprinted by permission of the publisher.

of Prophetic and Pharisaic Judaism and the Palestine of his day, the close of the period of the Second Temple. Hence it is somewhat strange to ask, What is Jesus to the Jews? "Jesus," says Wellhausen, "was not a Christian: he was a Jew," and, as a Jew, his life-story is that of one of the prominent men of the Jews of his time, while his teaching is Jewish teaching of a kind remarkable in its truth and its imaginativeness.

"Jesus was not a Christian," but he *became* a Christian. His teaching and his history have been severed from Israel. To this day the Jews have never accepted him, while his disciples and his followers of every generation have scoffed at and persecuted the Jews and Judaism. But even so, we cannot imagine a work of any value touching upon the history of the Jews in the time of the Second Temple which does not also include the history of Jesus and an estimate of his teaching. What, therefore, does Jesus stand for in the eyes of the Jews at the present time?

From the standpoint of general humanity he is, indeed, "a light to the Gentiles." His disciples have raised the lighted torch of the Law of Israel (even though that Law has been put forward in a mutilated and incomplete form) among the heathen of the four quarters of the world. No Jew can, therefore, overlook the value of Jesus and his teaching from the point of view of universal history. This was a fact which neither Maimonides nor Yehudah ha-Levi ignored.

But from the *national Hebrew* standpoint it is more difficult to appraise the value of Jesus. In spite of the fact that he himself was undoubtedly a "nationalist" Jew by instinct and even an extreme nationalist—as we may see from his retort to the Canaanitish woman, from his depreciatory way of referring to "the heathen and the publican," from the terms "Son of Abraham," "Daughter of Abraham" (which he uses as terms of the highest possible commendation), from his deep love for Jerusalem and from his devoting himself so entirely to the cause of "the lost sheep of the house of Israel" —in spite of all this, there was in him something out of which arose "non-Judaism."

What is Jesus to the *Jewish nation* at the present day?

To the Jewish nation he can be neither God nor the Son of God, in the sense conveyed by belief in the Trinity. Either conception is to the Jew not only impious and blasphemous, but incomprehensible. Neither can he, to the Jewish nation, be the

Messiah: the kingdom of heaven (the "Days of the Messiah") is not yet come. Neither can they regard him as a Prophet: he lacks the Prophet's political perception and the Prophet's spirit of national consolation in the political-national sense.

Neither can they regard him as a lawgiver or the founder of a new religion: he did not even desire to be such. Neither is he a *"Tanna,"* or Pharisaic rabbi: he nearly always ranged himself in opposition to the Pharisees and did not apprehend the positive side in their work, the endeavour to take within their scope the entire national life and to strengthen the national existence.

But Jesus is, for the Jewish nation, *a great teacher of morality and an artist in parable.* He is *the* moralist for whom, in the religious life, morality counts as everything. Indeed, as a consequence of this extremist standpoint his ethical code has become simply an ideal for the isolated few, a "Zukunfts Musik," an ideal for "the days of the Messiah," when an "end" shall have been made of this "old world," this present social order. It is no ethical code for the nations and the social order of to-day, when men are still trying to find the way to that future of the Messiah and the Prophets, and to the "kingdom of the Almighty" spoken of by the *Talmud,* an ideal which is of "this world" and which, gradually and in the course of generations, is to take shape in this world.

But in his ethical code there is a sublimity, distinctiveness and originality in form unparalleled in any other Hebrew ethical code; neither is there any parallel to the remarkable art of his parables. The shrewdness and sharpness of his proverbs and his forceful epigrams serve, in an exceptional degree, to make ethical ideas a popular possession. If ever the day should come and this ethical code be stripped of its wrappings of miracles and mysticism, the Book of the Ethics of Jesus will be one of the choicest treasures in the literature of Israel for all time.

JOEL CARMICHAEL: JESUS THE LEADER OF AN ARMED REVOLT [5]

Two rather sensational Jewish works on Jesus have appeared in the last two or three years. One is Carmichael's book on The Death of Jesus. *As a disciple of R. Eisler, he pictures Jesus as a Jewish revolutionary leader. Carmichael regards the Gospels*

[5] Joel Carmichael, *The Death of Jesus* (London: Pelican Books, 1966), pp. 131-133. Reprinted by permission of Victor Gollancz Ltd.

as on the whole an unhistorical concatenation of the dogmatic beliefs of the early Christian Church. Such few historical vestiges as they do contain, when extrapolated from the existing texts by diligent study, are seen to present Jesus as a political insurgent leading a militant group of zealot-like dissidents into armed conflict with the Roman occupiers of Palestine. His final downfall was brought about when at last he attempted a violent assault on the Jerusalem Temple.

However timeless Jesus' ethical message might have been—however timeless, that is, the ethical code of Judaism—he involved himself and his followers in an organized enterprise that had its roots in the circumstances of his own specific society. He had placed himself squarely in the long line of Jewish religious insurgents against the power of the idolatrous Roman state.

We can now see the climax of Jesus' career in an unexpected light; by entering Jerusalem with a group of armed men large enough, or powerful enough, or with enough popular support to overcome the defences of its headquarters, he arrogated sovereign power to himself. Whatever his own interpretation of this, whatever his specific motivation, whatever his ultimate purpose, this act of armed and organized violence was obviously bound to bring down on his head the swift retaliation of the Roman authorities.

From the Roman point of view, his being described on the cross as 'King of the Jews' was a simple statement of fact; there was nothing otherworldly for them about it at all—it referred to a basic act of insurrection, which was punished as such.

Nor was it only the Roman power that was threatened by Jesus' enterprise: the seizure of the Temple was directed just as much or more at the actual priesthood in charge of it, and, in a larger sense, doubtless at the entire Jewish aristocracy, which, however unwillingly, had become an outpost of the Roman state in Judea.

Thus, when Jesus' forces seized and held the Temple he fell foul of the Jewish aristocracy and of the priesthood. For while as indicated above he did not disapprove of the Temple cult *in principle*, and had no theory of reform, there was undoubtedly an element of social protest in his movement.

It would be rash to overemphasize the social teaching of someone who thought this world due for liquidation from one day to the next, but there is an undeniable note of indignation throughout the Gospels at the condition of the poor. It seems evident that Jesus was a prophet of the people; he represented the 'humble of Israel' and the *ammei ha-ares*. Within the framework of Judaism he was on the side of the downtrodden.

Hence it is more than likely that his attack on the Temple had the additional motivation of protest against social unrighteousness, as well as of a prophetically inspired aversion to the element of idolatry in the images on the Roman and other coins kept in the Temple. There is a revealing passage in Josephus that gives a startling picture of the oppression of the poor of the time by the rich, *via* the Temple: he reports that the insurgents wanted 'to destroy the moneylenders' tallies and to prevent the exaction of debts, in order to win over a host of grateful debtors and to rouse the poor against the wealthy with impunity.'

Indeed, the passage in *Mark* (6:8) expressly forbidding his disciples to carry money, and enjoining them to take nothing for their journey but a staff, with no bread, no bag, and no money in their belts, may even be a distorted recollection of Jesus' aversion to money *as such*.

In the Gospel account the genuine, compelling motives for the attack on the Temple have been blurred beyond recognition. The only things left are the banal slogans about the transformation of the 'universal house of prayer' into a 'den of burglars', as though it were a mere question of ethical theory divorced from the turbulence of the times. In the Synoptics generally, as a matter of fact, the chief motive underlying the resentment of the Temple authorities is given as Jesus' lack of a rabbinical education. The very simple-mindedness of this 'explanation' highlights the suppression of the authentic background of the Temple occupation.

The violence involved in the seizure of the Temple implies that it was deeply rooted in the social conflicts of the time, ideologized by religion as of course they were. The squeezing of the poorest classes by the middlemen interposed between them and the Temple hierarchy must have contributed to the explosive character of a movement that was bound to involve Jesus in a clash not only with the Romans but also with the Jewish aristocracy. The populace was exploited in the Temple, for instance, not only by its various exactions, but doubtless by such devices as a sliding scale of payments, in which the beasts bought by the pilgrims were assessed at a maximum price, while those who were selling animals for Temple disposition would always be told their animals had all sorts of blemishes making them unfit for sacrificial use.

The Temple, the unassailable and impregnable seat of socio-religious authority, must have provided parasitic priests and middlemen with an effective shield against any nonviolent popular protest. It was Jesus' attempt to smash this shield, as part of his larger enterprise of presiding over the installation of the Kingdom of God in defiance of the Roman power, that set in motion the events leading to his downfall.

Moreover, as we have seen, Jesus was entirely in harmony with the prophetic tradition, still alive in Israel, that had already completely spiritualized the relations of the Jews with their God. The entire Temple traffic in wine, oil, incense, wood, and animals for sacrifice might have seemed odious to him, at least in its exaggerated forms, whatever his acceptance of the Temple cult in principle.

Thus, his enterprise was bound to collide with the Roman and the Jewish authorities simultaneously even though Jesus thought himself a faithful interpreter of Judaism. The moment he resorted to action, as distinct from prophecy, he defied all institutional life and was, in fact, on the highroad to adventure.

The other Jewish book on Jesus of which notice was taken above is H. J. Schonfield's The Passover Plot *(London: Hutchinson and Co., 1965). It has a good deal in common with Carmichael's, at least to the extent that both picture Jesus as a rather swashbuckling man of action, an adventurer, and as one who "prayed and then got to work," as Schonfield puts it (p. 186). The work he did get to, in Schonfield's view, is, to put it mildly, quite intriguing—he was the instigator and perpetrator of an elaborate plot carried through in the Festival Week of Passover. By the most careful contrivance and timing he planned to have himself crucified and before death supervened to be brought down from the cross and by prearrangement laid in a tomb, from which he could be taken out and revived so as to give rise to the belief that he had come back from the dead. The main ingredients of this view are not new by any means; they are as old as the earliest Rationalist Lives of Jesus in the first part of the nineteenth century.*

The trouble with the works of Carmichael and Schonfield is that they do not take adequate notice of the apparently apolitical or suprapolitical aspect of Jesus' message on the kingdom of God, or of his refusal to describe its character and define the time of its coming. Moreover there is a grave inconsistency between Jesus the arch-revolutionary or Jesus the arch-conspirator of the Festival Week and the Jesus of the Sermon on the Mount. Presumably such books will continue to be written, and we should read them with as little passion as possible, assessing them against all the evidence of the Gospels. Certainly there is no gain for anyone in not daring to be honest about Jesus.

11

Scholarly Reconstructions of the Facts of Jesus' Life

In the last generation a number of very able and esteemed scholars of the New Testament have tried to avoid prejudging what the Gospels tell about Jesus from the angle of a particular theory concerning his life and mission. Instead they have attempted to reconstruct the facts of his life in their obscurity and complexity in as objective a manner as possible. To name a few, we mention Ch. Guignebert (France, 1933), M. Goguel (France, 1932 and 1950), M. Dibelius (Germany, 1939), V. Taylor (England, 1955), M. S. Enslin (America, 1961).

The problem here is that they all attempt to offer a biography *of Jesus in which the objective factual data of outward events or of the inner life of Jesus are strung together in connected chronological sequence. Against this it must be said that criticism of the Gospels in our time has made it ever clearer that these documents in fact conceal "the mind of Jesus" from us and do not give us a reliable chronology.*

Most scholars are agreed that contemporary materials including those from Qumrân may help to confirm or deny the historicity of this or that item in the Gospel tradition. Among contemporary scholars, two in particular, however, have made extensive use of sources extraneous to the Gospels in attempting to recover the historical Jesus, namely J. Jeremias of Göttingen and E. Stauffer of Erlangen. Jeremias calls upon Jewish sources and from an intensive study of their linguistic characteristics makes the sober estimate that the specific manner in which Abba, *Father and Amen at the head of a sentence are used in the New Testament must have been due to the individual creativeness of Jesus himself, and that these usages reflect his own sense of vocation,*[1] *as we noted in a previous section.*

[1] J. Jeremias, "The Present Position in the Controversy Concerning the Problem of the Historical Jesus," *The Expository Times,* **69** (August, 1958), 333-339.

Stauffer for his part ranges much further abroad and draws often much more fancifully on Roman as well as Jewish sources in his reconstruction of the facts about Jesus. Many would question whether, for instance, the story of the tribute money or the allusion in Luke 22:25 to Gentile rulers who let themselves be called "benefactors" (the title assigned to Alexander Balas on his silver coins according to Stauffer) really bears out Stauffer's emphatic statement that "Jesus' view of world-politics was far-reaching" (Jesus and His Story, *p. 55. See below*).

Stauffer maintains that a biography of Jesus is unattainable, and by "biography" he means a record of the psychological development of Jesus' life. What he is after is a history *of Jesus, and by that he means "the clear, strictly objective statement of those facts which can still be actually discerned" (p. 12). Now facts are facts and the historian cannot escape being concerned with them: they may even be intrinsically interesting. But it may be asked whether the essence of history has ultimately any more to do with external data and dates than the essence of mathematics has to do with numbers. If we are of the opinion that the history of Jesus is something more or something other than a collection of outward data empirically verified and set forth in chronological order, and that it consists rather of the interaction at the deepest personal level between Jesus and the folk he met in Judaea and Galilee, then we have every reason to be dissatisfied with Stauffer's treatment.*

The extract that follows from Stauffer about the star that appeared at Jesus' birth (Matthew 2:2) illustrates well his usual method of operation and how he sets about proving that it actually happened so. There will be some who find all this significant in itself or for the life of Jesus or for corroboration of the historical reliability of the Gospels, but few recent scholars of Jesus' life will set that much store by it.

E. STAUFFER: THE INFANT JESUS AND THE STAR [2]

'Where is he who has been born King of the Jews? For we have seen his star in the east and have come to worship him.' Thus spake the wise men from the east in Matt. 2.2. Perhaps Paul, too,

[2] E. Stauffer, *Jesus and His Story,* trans. Dorothea M. Barton (London: S.C.M. Press, 1960), pp. 36-38. Reprinted by permission of the publishers.

is thinking of the appearance of this star in Gal. 4.3f. At any rate, Ignatius of Antioch understood him to mean this when he combined the themes of Matt. 2 and Gal. 4 quite naturally in an apocalyptic advent hymn to the star of Bethlehem.

Kepler already applied the Matthaean text about the star at Bethlehem to the unique orbit of Jupiter in the year 7 B.C. In the spring of that year the planet Jupiter crossed the path of the planet Venus in the sky. In the summer and autumn of the same year Jupiter met the planet Saturn several times in the sign of the Fishes—the extremely rare *coniunctio magna,* which in this form occurs only every 794 years. According to the Matthaean account the magi had only observed the beginning of the planet's orbit, only the 'rise' of Jupiter, in the east, had based their astronomical and astrological forecast on this, had thereupon set out on their journey to Palestine, and had experienced there the crucial astral phenomenon (Matt. 2.9f.). It is known that the astronomers of antiquity observed and registered with the greatest attention all the movements in the starry heavens. Therefore the unusual nature of that conjunction of Jupiter could not have escaped them.

But was the science of astronomy in Jesus' day already in a position to calculate and forecast the orbits and conjunctions of the planets?

The answer is supplied by two new finds, the 'Berlin Table' of planets and the 'Star Almanac' of Sippar. The Berlin Table of planets is a tabulated list of the planetary movements in the near future, drawn up in the year 17 B.C. and covering the period to A.D. 10. It was copied on an Egyptian papyrus of A.D. 42. It proves that in those days the position of the stars could be calculated for decades ahead. The Star Almanac of Sippar is one of the latest cuneiform tablets which have been preserved. It is a prognostic planetary almanac for the year 7 B.C. which the ancient observatory of Sippar on the Euphrates—the Babylonian Greenwich—produced, probably at the end of the preceding year. On this clay tablet all the principal movements and crossings of the year are reckoned exactly to the month and the day. But the main theme is the conjunction of Jupiter and Saturn in the Fishes which is noted in advance about five times with exact dates. To sum up: *the science of astronomy of those days knew precisely what was approaching in the starry sky, and was looking forward with close attention particularly to the rare conjunction of Jupiter in the year 7* B.C.

What did contemporary astrology say about this heavenly phenomenon? We know about this too today. Jupiter was regarded as the star of the world ruler, and the constellation of the Fishes as the sign of the last days; the planet Saturn was considered in the east to be the star of Palestine. When Jupiter meets Saturn in the constellation of the Fishes, that signifies: *there will appear in Palestine in this year the ruler of the last days.* Now this is exactly the expectation which brought the wise men of Matt. 2.2 to Jerusalem.

It is clear that the Matthaean account stands on solid ground and agrees perfectly well with the original documents of the time. The clay tablet of Sippar is like an astronomical pocket almanac, of the kind with which the wise men from the east would have set out on their journey. There was good reason for their astrological deductions to cause some stir in Herodian Jerusalem.

No doubt the orbit of Jupiter of the year 7 B.C. was noticed and commented upon also in the Roman west. It is known that Augustus paid the greatest attention to the stellar phenomena, and the Berlin planetary table shows how exactly the movements of the stars were observed in Rome and Alexandria. In the Roman Empire Augustus was considered to be Jupiter in human form and ruler of the *ultima aetas.* Venus was regarded as the star of the Julian dynasty, and Saturn as the symbol of the Golden Age. The unusual orbit of Jupiter could thus, in the Roman empire in the year 7 B.C., point only to the career of the emperor Augustus. The year 7 must bring the glorious climax of this splendid career.

As a matter of fact we possess a whole series of documents from that time which supply direct or indirect evidence for this interpretation. One of these might be the Augustan inscription at Philae, of which no notice has so far been taken in this connexion. In the spring of the year 7 B.C. Jupiter crossed the path of the planet Venus which was considered in Egypt to be the star of Isis. On 8 March of that year an eminent citizen of Alexandria placed in the Isis temple on the island of Philae in the Nile a memorial tablet which extolled the emperor as *Zeus Eleutherios* and the star of the Greek world. We have discussed this elsewhere.

Thus the star of Bethlehem is a fact of history. But it is also a sign, as are all the events in the story of Jesus. Who was foretold by the phenomenon of the stars in 7 B.C.? Who is 'he who is to come'—*Augustus or Jesus?*

12
Existentialist Theologians Look at Jesus

The existentialist attitude in theology and New Testament interpretation, associated principally with the name of Rudolf Bultmann, has been highly influential for some time now. Bultmann's approach to the history of great individuals of the past like Jesus is diametrically opposed to the method of biographical reconstruction of external data noted in the preceding section. A man's history, for Bultmann, consists not of an outward sequence of events but of his inward aim, his intention, the drive and force of his life toward a specific goal.

We can see what is meant here by asking ourselves whether our curriculum vitae *divulges anything important about us—place and date of birth, formal education at school or college, employment. Does this say anything about what kind of person we are, about our "history"?*

Thus Bultmann insists (or insisted at an earlier stage of his career when he wrote his book on Jesus in 1925) that by way of the Gospels we can comprehend at least in part the "form of Jesus' being," the main thrust of his life, his "historical" contribution to the understanding of human existence.

Bultmann views Jesus as both eschatological preacher of the coming kingdom of God and rabbinic-type teacher of the will of God in the present. These two facets of his life are not incompatible, but are combined in him and result in his radical call to decision in the Now of his hearers' existence.

R. BULTMANN: JESUS AND THE NECESSITY OF DECISION [1]

The future Kingdom of God, then, is not something which is to come in the course of time, so that to advance its coming one can

[1] R. Bultmann, *Jesus and the Word, trans.* L. P. Smith and E. H. Lantero (New York: Charles Scribner's Sons, 1958), pp. 51-52. Reprinted by permission of the publisher.

do something in particular, perhaps through penitential prayers and good works, which become superfluous in the moment of its coming. Rather, the Kingdom of God is a power *which, although it is entirely future, wholly determines the present.* It determines the present because it now compels man to decision; he is determined thereby either in this direction or in that, as chosen or as rejected, in his entire present existence. Future and present are not related in the sense that the Kingdom begins as a historical fact in the present and achieves its fulfillment in the future; nor in the sense that an inner, spiritual possession of personal attributes or qualities of soul constitutes a present hold on the Kingdom, to which only the future consummation is lacking. Rather the Kingdom of God is genuinely future, because it is not a metaphysical entity or condition, but the future action of God, which can be in no sense something given in the present. None the less this future determines man in his present, and exactly for that reason is true future—not merely something to come "somewhere, sometime," but destined for man and constraining him to decision.

The coming of the Kingdom of God is therefore not really an event in the course of time, which is due to occur sometime and toward which man can either take a definite attitude or hold himself neutral. Before he takes any attitude he is already constrained to make his choice, and therefore he must understand that just this necessity of decision constitutes the essential part of his human nature. Because Jesus sees man thus in a crisis of decision before God, it is understandable that in his thought the Jewish Messianic hope becomes the absolute certainty that in this hour the Kingdom of God is coming. If men are standing in the crisis of decision, and if precisely this crisis is the essential characteristic of their humanity, then every hour is the last hour, and we can understand that for Jesus the whole contemporary mythology is pressed into the service of this conception of human existence. Thus he understood and proclaimed his hour as the last hour.

This message of the Kingdom of God is absolutely alien to the present-day conception of humanity. We are accustomed to regard a man as an individual of the species "man," a being endowed with definite capacities, the development of which brings the human ideal in him to realization—of course with variations in each individual. As "character" or as "personality," man achieves his end. Harmonious development of all human faculties, according to the individual endowment of each man, is the way to this ideal. Perhaps no man can travel this road to the end, but progress along the road, bringing the ideal nearer to realization, justifies human existence. We are accustomed to distinguish between the physical or sensuous and the mental or spiritual life. And even if at the same time the connection between them is assumed, and symmetrical development is the shining goal, still the spirit is the guiding principle, and the life of the spirit is the true meaning of human existence.

All this is completely alien to the teaching of Jesus. Jesus expresses no conception of a human ideal, no thought of a development of human capacities, no idea of something valuable in man as such, no conception of the spirit in the modern sense. Of the spirit in our sense and of its life or experience, Jesus does not speak at all. The word which in the English Biblical translations is generally rendered "soul" or "spirit" usually means simply "life," as in the well-known saying: "What shall it profit a man if he gains the whole world and loses his soul?" (Mark 8:36) The meaning is simply: Of what use are all the possessions of the world to a man who must die?

G. BORNKAMM: JESUS' DEMAND TO LOVE[2]

Bornkamm, who studied under Bultmann, discounts like his teacher all attempts to comprehend the historical Jesus along biographical or psychological lines. His Jesus of Nazareth, *to which we have referred before, is by no means a Life —for him a Life is impossible on the basis of the Gospel sources. But it is not impossible to take hold of the "history" of Jesus in the deeper sense in which the Gospels speak of it as an event of unmistakeable distinctiveness. And Bornkamm finds the "essence" of the event of Jesus to lie in the fact that in his words and deeds God confronts his hearers just where they are with the immediacy of his presence and of his radical claim upon them.*

As never before the story of the Good Samaritan makes it plain that true love cannot justify or spare a corner for self-love, and knows no reserve, not even towards an enemy. All too frequently

[2] G. Bornkamm, *op. cit.*, pp. 114-115.

our use of the expression "acting the Good Samaritan" arises from the acts of charity described in the tale. Originally, however, the statement of the man's nationality is intended to bring out the natural relationship of inborn arch-enmity between him and the Jew overtaken by misfortune. But this no longer applies. Love breaks through the boundaries––fortified as they are by age-old religious and social history and, to all appearances, impenetrable.

Jesus never bases this claim of love upon a universal idea of God, or upon an enlightened view of the national and religious questions at issue between Jews and Samaritans. Nor does he base it upon some such conception of man, say as is taught by the Stoics, to the effect that man as such is sacred (*homo res sacra homini,* Seneca Ep. 95, 33). Nor is his commandment to love our enemies concerned with achieving a pedagogical effect upon the other or with our own self-discipline. The ground of his command of love is simply because it is what God wills and what God does. That is the meaning of the passage: "So if you are offering your gift at the altar, and there remember that your brother has something against you, leave your gift there before the altar and go; first be reconciled to your brother, and then come and offer your gift" (Mt. v. 23). For God is prepared to wait, and does not want men to come to him alone, unreconciled. Reconciliation to him without a readiness to be reconciled to your brother is impossible. The fifth petition of the Lord's Prayer puts it similarly: "Forgive us our debts as we also have forgiven our debtors" (Mt. vi. 12). God makes no difference between friend and foe. "For he makes his sun to rise on the evil and on the good, and sends rain on the just and on the unjust" (Mt. v. 45). Therefore, the bridges between man and man, although they may appear to have been destroyed a thousand times through wrong-doing, denunciation and persecution, are never broken down in God's sight. Even the persecuted and the abused is not relieved of his duty: "Love your enemies; do good to those who hate you, bless those who curse you, pray for those who abuse you" (Lk. vi. 27f.).

The fact that love has no limits does not imply the vague boundlessness of some concept of mankind. The natural divisions between friend and foe, between Jew and Samaritan, neighbour and stranger, Pharisee and tax collector, righteous and unrighteous, are certainly everywhere presupposed, and not ignored; but love penetrates these frontiers for God's sake and for our brother's sake, for whom I have a responsibility from which God does not release me.

Hence Jesus' answer to Peter's question: "Lord, how often shall my brother sin against me, and I forgive him? As many as seven times?" "I do not say to you seven times, but seventy times seven" (Mt. xviii. 21f.).

Afterword: The Mystery of Jesus' Person and History

In the beginning of *The Divine Propagandist,* Lord Beaverbrook writes: "The teachings of Jesus should not be dealt with exclusively by preachers and scholars. It is the right of the man who has lived in the market place to outline the sermons of Christ as he conceives them. . . . I reject all pretensions to higher criticism. I tell in brief form and plain terms some of the simple facts of Jesus' life on earth." [1]

The honesty in that is admirable and the contention largely justified. Biblical experts have no monopoly of knowledge of Jesus. Nor is such knowledge entirely dependent on the learned doctors or professors. The word of any single scholar or group of scholars should not be taken as the last word. The plain man *has* a plain right, on reading the Gospels, to conceive his own "image" of the man of Nazareth.

All the same to neglect the long and ongoing process of scholarly criticism of the Gospels is to run the risk of lapsing into false assumptions or of yielding to subjective flights of fancy, whereby we make of Jesus just what we want him to be. The whole venture of critical study of the Gospels should act as a balance, a control on us. Any startlingly new solution to the problem of Jesus that takes no account of the best results of criticism is not likely to be anything but startlingly absurd. In the business of investigating Jesus' life we can only build for the future on insights inherited from those who have gone before us. Here supremely, as in all historical enquiry, patience, discipline and a sense of indebtedness to the devoted labors of our forebears are great virtues.

Little has been said in this book about the claims made for Jesus or the divine honors accorded to him by Christian believers after his death and resurrection. Believers in the early Church could not speak of God without also and at the same time naming Jesus. Why and how did they do so? Were they in on the truth about this man? These questions carry us over into the realm of faith and

[1] Lord Beaverbrook, *op. cit.,* p. 1.

theology. In the question of whether the Gospels are "true" in their overall portrayal of Jesus, faith and theology are ultimately involved. The historian's verdict does not decide this issue. It is one thing to prove the Gospels "true," it is another to show by historical research that this or that miracle, saying, or act of Jesus does or does not go back to him at all and is therefore historical or unhistorical.

As historians, we find a good many features in the Gospels that do not appear to represent the original facts. We find just as many others about which we can only confess our continuing uncertainty. But sooner or later, if we are really open-minded, we also run across this assured datum of history, that a man by the name of Jesus appeared among his contemporaries and confronted them in their own concrete situation with a dimension beyond their world, with God.

Today some radical theologians wish to abolish talk of God, and they are at liberty to do so. They believe that the word "God" has no referent and is accordingly meaningless. Yet they remain tremendously interested in Jesus of Nazareth. They describe him variously as "the uniquely free man," "the man for others," "the fall guy in the profane world." In other words, they want to speak of Jesus as though for him too God-language were no part of his life and history. The trouble here is that they thus transgress their proper limits and betray genuine historical perspective. For in point of fact Jesus did use God-talk. However meaningless the word "God" may be for some in our generation, it certainly was not so for him. He did direct men away from himself to God.

Whatever further illumination on Jesus may come to us from future study, the historian will always have to take account of this, that Jesus affirmed: "God will reign."

Bibliographical Note

The purpose of this note is to draw attention again to works mentioned only in passing in the text, but principally to add a list of important supplementary readings. The list has to be very selective and is confined to works available in English. All the books mentioned in the preceding pages should of course be taken as basic readings. So also should the Gospels, and these should be consulted in both the Revised Standard Version and the New English Bible.

Whereas the quest of the historical Jesus began to arise only in the late eighteenth and early nineteenth centuries, R. M. Grant's *The Earliest Lives of Jesus* (London, 1961) seeks to show that early Church Fathers like Clement of Alexandria and Origen were at least tentatively interested in historical problems relating to Jesus. But their main concern was an ancient and prescientific concern with Jesus as the divine logos.

Studies in the background of the New Testament and early Christianity both on the Greco-Roman or Hellenistic side and on the Jewish side are important for an understanding of the life of Jesus. W. P. Hatch's *The Influence of Greek Ideas on Christianity* (New York: Harper Torchbooks, 1957) is now old but still standard. A. D. Nock, *Early Gentile Christianity and Its Hellenistic Background* (New York: Harper Torchbooks, 1964) is indispensable, although as its title suggests it bears more, like the previous book, on nascent Christianity than on Jesus. The same is true of the useful and admirable collection of Roman-Hellenistic readings in C. K. Barrett, ed., *The New Testament Background: Selected Documents* (New York: Harper Torchbooks, 1961); see also F. C. Grant, *Roman Hellenism and the New Testament* (London, 1962).

Books on the Palestinian-Jewish background are more directly pertinent to the life of Jesus. Helpful and fairly non-technical accounts of ancient Judaism are the following: F. C. Grant, *Ancient Judaism and the New Testament* (New York, 1959); W. Foerster, *From the Exile to Christ,* translated by G. E. Harris (Philadelphia, 1964). Among basic texts on the Qumrân sect and Scrolls are T. H. Gaster's translation of the major documents of Qumrân, T. H. Gaster, *The Dead Sea Scriptures in English Translation* (New York, 1957); also F. M. Cross Jr., *The Ancient Library of Qumrân,* revised edition (New York, 1961); Matthew Black, *The Scrolls and Christian Origins* (New York, 1961). For a series of interesting essays on special subjects relating to Qumrân Judaism and Judaism in general and the New Testament, see K. Stendahl, ed., *The Scrolls and the New Testament* (New York, 1957) and W. D. Davies, *Christian Origins and Judaism* (London, 1962). R. Bultmann, *Primitive Christianity in Its Contemporary Setting,* translated by R. H. Fuller (New York and London, 1956), deals with the Jewish background but gives special attention to Gnosticism. On Gnosticism see also F. C. Burkitt, *The Church and Gnosis* (Cambridge, 1932), and a more recent study taking the recent finds at Chenoboskion into consideration, R. McL. Wilson, *The Gnostic Problem* (London, 1958). The student of the life and times of Jesus should also be familiar with the Jewish apocryphal and apocalyptic literature of the Intertestamental period, for which consult R. H. Charles, *The Apocrypha and Pseudepigrapha,* 2 vols. (Oxford, 1913).

Among exponents of the Christ-myth theory, mentioned at the beginning of the present book in connection with the name of Paul-Louis Couchoud, are also A. Drews, *The Witnesses to the Historicity of Jesus,* translated by J. McCabe (London, 1910); A. Kalthoff, *The Rise of Christianity,* translated from the German (London, 1907), the latter presenting a Marxist account of Christian origins.

Among the most influential of English Lives of Jesus in the nineteenth century was that by F. W. Farrar, *The Life of Christ* (London, Paris and New York, 1874). In the early years of this century a crop of Lives appeared which took up in one way or another the ideas of Strauss or Renan, e.g. Sir J. R. Seeley, *Ecce Homo* (London, 1900); Oscar Holtzmann, *The Life of Jesus,* translated by J. T. Bealby and M. A. Canney (London, 1904); W. Bousset, *Jesus,* translated by J. P. Trevelyan, edited by W. D. Morrison (London, 1906); D. Smith, *The Days of His Flesh* (London, 1907).

Among more recent scholarly reconstructions which seek to avoid modernizing Jesus and to present the course of his life as objectively as possible, the following are some of the most important: Charles Guignebert, *Jesus,* translated by S. H. Hooke (London, 1935); M. Dibelius, *Jesus* (London, 1939); V. Taylor, *The Life and Ministry of Jesus* (London, 1955); M. S. Enslin, *The Prophet from Nazareth* (New York, 1961).

Of the countless works dealing with special themes relating to Jesus, only one or two belonging to the main categories can be mentioned here.

Among works dealing with the process of transmission of the Gospel tradition and its compilation in the Gospels, the following should be studied as leading works in Form-criticism: R. Bultmann, *The History of the Synoptic Tradition,* translated by John Marsh (New York and Evanston, 1963). M. Dibelius, *From Tradition to Gospel,* translated in collaboration with the author by B. L. Woolf (New York, 1965). For English attitudes to the tradition sympathetic to Form-criticism, see R. H. Lightfoot, *History and Interpretation in the Gospels* (London, 1935) and also *The Gospel Message of St. Mark* (Oxford, 1950); also D. E. Nineham, *The Gospel of St. Mark* (London, 1963). For the other side of the picture consult V. Taylor, *The Formation of the Gospel Tradition* (London, 1935) and also the Introduction in his commentary on Mark, *The Gospel According to St. Mark* (London, 1952).

Reference was made in a previous section of this volume to Redaction-criticism. Whereas Form-criticism sets out to analyze the form and content of single or isolated sayings and narratives in the Gospels, Redaction-criticism is the study of the overall framework or pattern of each Gospel as a whole in order to learn the intention of each Evangelist in composing his Gospel as he has done. There has lately been a growing recognition that the Evangelists were not merely scissors-and-paste editors of the traditions that were handed on to them, but theologians in their own right, and that in the alterations or redactions they make in the sources they use they reveal their theological aims in relation to their presentation of Jesus. Three books of this kind may be mentioned here: H. Conzelmann, *The Theology of St. Luke,* translated by G. Buswell (London, 1960); J. M. Robinson, *The Problem of History in Mark* (London, 1957); G. Bornkamm, G. Barth and H. J. Held, *Tradition and Interpretation in Matthew,* translated by Percy Scott (London, 1963).

On the general subject of the teaching of Jesus one of the standard works is that by T. W. Manson, *The Teaching of Jesus* (Cambridge 1939). The most recent treatment is by Norman Perrin, *Rediscovering the Teaching of Jesus* (New York, 1967). The parables in particular have recently been the subject of intensive investigation: see C. H. Dodd, *The Parables of the Kingdom* (London, 1941); also the highly influential work of J. Jeremias, *The Parables of Jesus,* translated by S. H. Hooke, revised edition (New York, 1963). N. Perrin, *The Kingdom of God in the Teaching of Jesus* (London, 1963), presents a valuable critical survey of the history of interpretation of Jesus' message on the kingdom, and makes his own contribution.

Helpful correctives to popular misunderstandings of the miracles are offered by A. Richardson, *The Miracle Stories of the Gospels* (London, 1941) and R. H. Fuller, *Interpreting the Miracles* (London, 1963).

Popular studies of Jesus' ethic informed by sound critical scholarship are: E. F. Scott, *The Ethical Teaching of Jesus* (London, 1924) and John Knox, *The Ethic of Jesus in the Teaching of the Church* (New York, Nashville, 1961). More technical but especially important is the study by A. N. Wilder, *Eschatology and Ethics in the Teaching of Jesus* (New York, 1950). H. K. McArthur's *Understanding the Sermon on the Mount* (New York, 1960) presents a summary of various interpretations of the Sermon, and W.D. Davies' *The Setting of the Sermon on the Mount* (Cambridge, 1964) provides an exhaustive study of the literary structure and relationships and historical background of the Sermon.

A short work first published in 1892 by the German pietist theologian Martin Kähler, *The So-called Historical Jesus and the Historic, Biblical Christ,* translated and edited by Carl E. Braaten (Philadelphia, 1964), has figured prominently in recent discussion. Kähler holds that the only true Jesus Christ is the total biblical Christ who is the preached Christ, not the Jesus whose life is reconstructed by the modern historians. The various books of John Knox lucidly demonstrate the difficulties involved in trying to recover the life of Jesus from the Gospels and emphasize that the event of Jesus Christ does not consist of Jesus in isolation but of Jesus as responded to and interpreted by his followers both before and after his death; e.g. John Knox, *Criticism and Faith* (London, 1953) and also *The Death of Christ: The Cross in New Testament History and Faith* (New York, 1958).

In regard to the question of the relation of the historical Jesus to the Christ proclaimed by the Church, the question of the Christological titles used by Jesus in the Gospels or applied to him is crucial. On these titles see: V. Taylor, *The Names of Jesus* (London, 1954); O. Cullmann, *The Christology of the New Testament,* translated by S. C. Guthrie and C. A. M. Hall (Philadelphia, 1959); A. J. B. Higgins, *Jesus and the Son of Man* (London, 1964); H. E. Tödt, *The Son of Man in the Synoptic Tradition,* translated by Dorothea M. Barton (London, 1965); and R. H. Fuller, *The Foundations of New Testament Christology* (New York, 1965). See also William Manson, *Jesus the Messiah* (Philadelphia, 1946) and T. W. Manson, *The Servant Messiah* (Cambridge, 1953).

J. M. Robinson's programmatic essay, *A New Quest of the Historical Jesus* (London, 1959), is the classic statement of the factors leading to the decline of the old quest of the historical Jesus, the partial eclipse of interest in Jesus under the impact of first Barth's and then Bultmann's theology, and the rise of the so-called "new quest" since 1953. The "new quest" has produced an extensive literature mainly in the learned journals. For other surveys relating to this "new quest" see H. Zahrnt, *The Historical Jesus,* translated by J. S. Bowden (London, 1963), and H. Anderson, *Jesus and Christian Origins, A Commentary on Modern Viewpoints* (New York, 1964).

Among works stemming from the Bultmann group of scholars, i.e. those who were former students of Bultmann, the following are good examples of the existentialist tendency in the study of Jesus: E. Käsemann's essay on "The Problem of the Historical Jesus" in *Essays on New Testament Themes,* translated by W. Montague (Naperville, 1964); the series of rather specialized and technical studies by E. Fuchs, *Studies of the Historical Jesus,* translated by A. Scobie (Naperville, 1964). Käsemann and Fuchs, in pleading for a renewed interest in the historical Jesus, are concerned less with reconstruction of the factual data of his life than with the question of the connection between the preacher and teacher, Jesus of Nazareth, and the preached Christ of the Church's faith.

Index